About Meditation

Carl Mohan

CONTENTS

Introduction
The Quest for Truth   01

Part One: In the Beginning
A Creation Story   05
I AM   10
Happiness   12

Part Two: Attitude
The Approach   15
The Journey   17
What Lies Beneath   20

Part Three: Preparation   21

Part Four: Purpose   25

Part Five: Duality   31

ABOUT MEDITATION

Part Six: Stillness	37
Part Seven: The Embracing Life Force	44
Part Eight: Follow Me	51
Part Nine: The Inner Voice	54
Samuel	59
Part Ten: Dreams	60
Sleep	63
The Cosmos	64
Part Eleven: Love	65
The Paradigm of Love	69
Part Twelve: Truth	71
Part Thirteen: Fear	76
Part Fourteen: Death	84
Part Fifteen: Rebirth	88
Birth	95
Part Sixteen: Being	97

Part Seventeen: Forgiveness	100
Part Eighteen: The Book of Errors	106
The Light of the Heart	113
Part Nineteen: Healing	114
Part Twenty: Light	
Light Which Defines Life	124
Crown of Light	126
Part Twenty-one: On the Road to Victory	128
Part Twenty-two: Meditate Upon the Light Within	
Guided Imagery	133
Preparation	135
Prayer of Bliss	142
Part Twenty-three: Crystal Light Meditation	
Preparation	144
Crystal Light Meditation	146
Reflection	153
Questions	157
The Nature of Life	157
Faith	163
The Unknown Question	164
The Answer	167

Manifesting Light   169
Freedom   171
Moments   174
Mastery of Life   174

Part Twenty-four: On Being a Master   177

Afterword
About Books of Interest   182
Dawn   193

APPENDICES

Appendix A: Life Force Chart   194

Appendix B: Exercises   195
Exercise One – Planting Intentions
Exercise Two – Natural Rhythms
Exercise Three – Intentions
Exercise Four – Remembering Happiness
Exercise Five – Choosing Happiness
Exercise Six – Reveal Karma
Exercise Seven – Daily Prayer
Exercise Eight – Walk Each Day
Exercise Nine – Planting Light Buds
Exercise Ten – Meditate Daily

Appendix C: Light Buds   201

Bibliography   208

The End   210

*The Mastery of Self
Through*

Meditations for the Journey into Light

*Answers to life's questions are like seeds
Seeds of light which you plant within
Nurture them
And they will blossom
To Illumine you*

About Meditation

Carl Mohan

Edgar Cayce Readings © 1971, 1993-2007 by The Edgar Cayce Foundation. All Rights Reserved.

The King James Version of the Holy Bible, *eBook edition*, Project Gutenberg, Public Domain, USA, 1989.

Copyright © 2022 Carl Mohan

All rights reserved. No part of this publication may be reproduced or transmitted in any form or by any means, graphic, mechanical, electronic, including photocopying, recording, taping, information storage or retrieval systems, or otherwise, without prior written approval from the author.

ISBN: 978-0-9782970-1-5 PRINT
ISBN: 978-0-9782970-5-3 EPUB
ISBN: 978-0-9782970-4-6 MOBI

Carl Mohan
Guelph, Ontario, Canada
vision.dreamer@yahoo.ca

This book is dedicated to my friend Keith. He does not ascribe to my belief system but is, nonetheless, a paragon of his own beliefs. Anyone who can demonstrate such commitment has exceeded that state of simply being a parent and member of a society. When you have found someone whose life is worthy of emulation, you have found someone who walks as a teacher in the truest sense.

CARL MOHAN

As the inquiring mind seeks
Meditation will offer answers
Which inspire a new path

ACKNOWLEDGEMENTS

Our lives are shaped by choices. My life choices were influenced by my parents, society, economics, and the church. My inquisitive nature led me to various other sources and teachers. When I was young, the works of *Edgar Cayce (1877–1945)*, an American clairvoyant, helped form the foundation of my mental framework. I was also inspired by the teachings found in the King James version of the *Holy Bible*, but during my childhood I began to realize those teachings could not be taken at face value. To find the truth, the words needed interpretation.

My quest for truth introduced me to various other authors and teachers and it is through these personal experiences that I came to understand the real meanings of Truth and Love as well as their connection with a higher state of happiness. With these reflections in mind, I hope the writings herein help others in their own quest for truth.

I wish to express gratitude to my wife, three children, multiple friends (and some unfriendly connections), for being sources of inspiration.

Preface

"When I was a child, I spake as a child, I understood as a child, I thought as a child: but when I became a man, I put away childish things." (1 Corinthians 13:11, Holy Bible, King James Version).

When I was a child, my mind was filled with awe and wonder about the nature of everything. I wondered at my own place in the grand scheme of life. Logic told me to seek parallels with animal life, but it didn't feel right. People had to be something different. At the time, I did not realize I was attaining the awareness of my own consciousness or ego. I felt that human life was something greater and different from the animals. I saw four legs and animal personalities, but I was different and could not associate any part of my being with the animal kingdom. I knew I had to be different but did not know how. I would lay on the cold concrete walkway at the back of my parents' house, gaze at the blue sky, float with the clouds, and wonder. More thoughts and questions would fill my inquiring mind.

I looked at the trees and the birds and all the magnificent creations, and marvelled at them. I felt there must be an intelligence behind the grand design; there must be a higher power or God that was responsible for it all.

Being born into a Presbyterian family meant attending church was part of my upbringing. From an early age, I realized teachers and ministers of religion did not understand what they were preaching. They pointed up for God and mouthed empty words attempting to sound pious. It did not feel right. I did not see Truth in the dogma being regurgitated. I was hungry for understanding and this was not the source. It was frustrating.

Nevertheless, the *Holy Bible* became an important book in my life. From an early age, I realized a deeper meaning behind the words. For example, the *Book of Revelation* is not simply a prediction of gloom and doom, but instead, it describes the relationship between Spirit and the flesh which it enlivens. It offers an understanding of who we are and how we function as spiritual beings in the physical world. The seeker can find understanding by interpreting the message like a dream. We will leave the subject of Revelation here since the focus of this book is meditation.

ABOUT MEDITATION

When I was young, tools such as the internet did not exist. My only source for Truth about life came from parents and the church. As a child, this formed the framework of my mind. The opportunity to disconnect from that framework came when I migrated to another country and entered university. My inquiring mind continued exploring beyond the boundaries of traditional thought.

I was a free thinker and my life was an open book. I could do whatever I wanted and could navigate my life in whatever direction I chose. The power of parents or church no longer controlled my life. The world was my stage and I could write whatever drama I chose for my life.

At the time, I did not have the wisdom to stand aside, look at the options before me, and choose wisely. Instead, I was like a boat floating on a river. I moved with the water, sometimes turbulent and sometimes calm. My life was under the control of the current. Many opportunities and ideas came my way, but without a specific purpose or objective, life meandered until I learnt that the practice of meditation offered answers.

It is easy to look back at life and see where I have been and the paths which led to where I am now. I could trace my steps based on the choices made along the way. There were many instances where my choices resulted in happiness and enlightenment.

For example, choosing to live in the country brought happiness and peace of mind. Visiting the Lily Dale Spiritualist Community opened doors that led to places which I would have never imagined otherwise. I met people who offered guidance that opened my eyes to the amazing inner world of the Life Force. Some were lucrative, such as opening a computer business, while others were not. I always regretted turning down a few people that were interested in joining my business ventures. Later in life, I realized that their skills would have greatly enhanced the business. I could have chosen different paths and my life would have been engineered differently. The result would have been a totally different mental, spiritual, emotional and physical framework.

However, it is what it is, and I am who I am because of my choices. I feel it incumbent upon myself to record all I have learnt during my journey so that others might learn from what I have gathered along the way. Hopefully they can avoid the mistakes I have made and create a framework, bounded by conscious choice, based on the wisdom that yields the greatest form of happiness, the mastery of life, or something even greater—Love.

Love fills the crucible of Truth. It is Love which manifests a life of possibilities—one of which creates the adventure of happiness.

INTRODUCTION
The Quest for Truth

Truth, which enlightens the mind, can be found in many places and in various ways. Meditation, Indigenous ceremony, and the Hindu form of Yoga, are examples which are practiced today. Meditation—the subject of this book—is found in sacred texts such as the *Holy Bible, The Quran, The Vedas, The Upanishads, Bhagavad Gita*, and the *Tipitaka*. In these texts, Truth can be found if one is willing to look beyond the filters of society. Truth is all-encompassing. It applies to all and everything, regardless of the source. Later in this book, I explain how the greatest form of Truth emerges from within.

Finding Truth in today's society requires weeding through societal chaff. Examples from the *Holy Bible* are used in this book, but the practice of meditation is not dependent on any religion or organized belief systems. As noted above, Truth emerges from within.

The society in which we live is represented by people scarred by a history of indoctrination. Governments, churches, and industry all play a role in shaping attitudes and expectations. Many of the churches in western society preach meaningless dogma instead of Truth. Governments use misinformation and fear to erode the freedom of the individual. Industries use the media as a conditioning tool so people will buy products. The internet is used to frame false information as Truth and present it to a vast audience. Education systems are designed to perpetuate patterns of conditioning. Children are taught how to think and what to think, and when they reach adulthood, continue to teach these patterns to succeeding generations. For example, they may pass on the idea that the inner motivating force, or free will, should be ignored and replaced with ideas and attitudes which conform to society. Consequently, personal freedoms are eroded with the perpetuation of false philosophies such as "the good of the many outweighs the good of the few" and this is incentivized using scenarios of fear.

Generations of this type of conditioning has resulted in the mental framework of people today. Populations have become locked into societal slavery where life is directed by external conditioning instead of inner motivation. The resulting hierarchical societies overshadow the truth that each individual's life is equally precious and should be treated as such. A closer look will reveal that personal growth is not part of the picture. Society is not designed for the benefit of the individual.

The concept of a self-directed life, where an individual can embrace complete mental, spiritual, physical, and emotional potential, has become foreign. Seekers have failed to find answers through traditional avenues. Instead, they have found only systems which diminish the significance of the individual.

Resistance is NOT futile. Weeding through societal chaff will reveal that the practice of meditation can be used by anyone to find meaningful answers to life's questions. In mainstream society, meditation is often viewed as a method of relaxation, and it can indeed work for this purpose. However, it is much more than that. The meditative state offers a view of life with objectivity and detachment from controlling doctrines. It can also be used to discover and harness the untapped essence of life connected to the true self. The practice can open the door to the truest form of freedom: that is, a life directed by inner guidance.

The practice of meditation can be used to access the dynamics of life, make changes, and restore the natural equilibrium between the Life Force and the psyche, mind, body, and consciousness. The meditative process involves accessing inner recesses of the psyche where untapped abilities are revealed. The process of incorporating all of it into everyday life can be considered a journey. In the early chapters, elementary steps are first introduced, followed by the types of experiences, knowledge, and wisdom that may be encountered. Later chapters demonstrate how the experiences can be incorporated into everyday life to facilitate growth and change.

Practitioners will gain clarity on how to untangle connections from the past which have resulted in their current state of being. Furthermore, it will become possible to open a door to a future where life can be embraced to the fullest; one on a trajectory to mental, spiritual, physical, and emotional happiness. The current holding pattern, which has resulted from societal slavery, will be dissolved. Following the spiritual guidance offered through the practice of meditation, balance will be restored between the physical and Life Force, liberating the true self to experience physical and non-physical mastery.

If you are prepared to embark on a journey to uncover eternal Truths, experience the purest form of Love, and achieve full potential, then sit back and buckle up for the ride of your life.

PART ONE
In the Beginning

A Creation Story

How did it all come into being? Creation resulted from Light which entered the dark realms and manifested life. Brilliant, exciting, exhilarating, magnificent, wonderful, joyous, and mighty are words which cannot adequately describe feelings which this Light manifests. This Light is everywhere, here on earth and all the realms of creation.

Before this Light emerged, it stands to reason that darkness was everywhere, not only on Earth, but throughout the entire cosmos and every corner which the mind can fathom. Ancient documents suggest that darkness existed before the onset of Light. For example, the second verse in the *Holy Bible* explains, *"and darkness was upon the face of the deep." (Genesis 1:2, Holy Bible, King James Version)*.

Taking this thought one step further, the creator of Light and the darkness must exist somewhere outside of its creations. Simple as it may sound, all that exists and the realms from which existence emerged cannot be fully fathomed by the human mind. The mind's inquiring nature however, will seek an understanding of human life and will be propelled by an innate desire to find the source, purpose and reason for its existence.

It is clear that the creator of Light and dark held the power to manifest existence as we know it. The inquiring mind would try to formulate questions regarding the nature of this force. Logic would suggest that it would have many facets, one of which exudes thoughts that result in creation as we know it *(Genesis 1-2, the Holy Bible, King James Version)*.

When the mind tries to understand the creator, it will not succeed. This is simply because the mind cannot see beyond the boundaries of its own existence. In other words, the mind is part of the dynamics of creation, beyond which it is unable to explore.

Imagine total darkness—a moment where there is an absolute absence of light. Imagine a place within the depths of space far beyond the reaches of the sunlight, or any light. Imagine the feeling of absolute nothingness which the total darkness generates. It is within this realm that light entered. One can only imagine the nature of the thoughts from the creative force which manifested the Light that neutralized darkness. Light is the force which creates, while darkness, nothingness, and emptiness were the precursor. Light is the instrument of the Life Force which manifests life here on Earth.

It is the Light of the creator which shines through the cells of the human body in order to animate physical life. The human body is an instrument of the Light, experiencing a slice of time within the landscape of eternity. This interval of time occurs in a place where there was once darkness. The earth too is a creation of Light. It is a place of powerful emotions which the Light can experience and explore through human life. It can explore the full potential of the earth's environment through the facilities of the physical body.

Logic would suggest to the inquiring mind that darkness was neutralized by a creative force so that it may experience the various realms. What is the difference between the light which is seen through physical eyes and the Light shining from the creator within the realms? The mind can rationalize both concepts where one is viewed as a mirror of the other. The light from the sun provides energy to create an environment capable of sustaining life, while the Light of the creator enlivens its creations in order to experience all the aspects of life within the realm.

The sun pours energy onto the earth in a very fine balance, creating an environment suitable for various forms of life. It is the same for other planets in the solar system. They all sustain life in various forms resulting from the nature of the energy shining from the sun in conjunction with the Light from the creator. It is only logical.

The light of the sun can offer a view of the physical realm through eyes of flesh, while the Light of the Spirit, creator force or Life Force can offer a different perspective, one of the spiritual-world viewed through inner eyes or the eyes of the Spirit. Light from the sun fills physical eyes with a reflection of physical reality. Out of nothingness, Light, which the physical eyes cannot perceive, is the substance of the Spirit. It neutralizes darkness wherever it is present, manifesting thoughts as expressions of life, such as human existence.

A force so powerful and amazing, one which is incomprehensible by the mind, journeyed into its creation through the enlightened physical body—this was the first journey into Light. Here on Earth, the enlightened being was free to choose and experience. Happiness was the natural state until the free will to choose guided life in a different direction. Exercising of the free will to choose for the first time can be found in the first book of the *Holy Bible*. *"And the LORD God commanded the man, saying, Of every tree of the garden thou mayest freely eat: But of the tree of the knowledge of good and evil, thou shalt not eat of it." (Genesis 2:16-17, Holy Bible, King James Version). "And when the woman saw that the tree was good for food, and that it was pleasant to the eyes, and a tree to be desired to make one wise, she took off the fruit thereof, and did eat, and gave also unto her husband with her; and he did eat." Genesis 3:6, Holy Bible, King James Version).*

Free will navigated human life away from its true enlightened nature, away from its brilliant, exciting, exhilarating, magnificent, wonderful, joyous, and mighty existence, and away from the happiness that could have been fully experienced.

CARL MOHAN

I AM

I am a light.
I am a light shining from the depths of the Universe.
I am a light shining from the depths of the universe
here to have a physical experience.
I am a light shining from the depths of the universe
here to experience the experience of experience.
I am a light that embraced the cells of this earth.
I am a light that borrowed the cells of this earth
to experience the physical.

I came.
I saw.
I hungered.

I felt the emotions.
I felt the desire.
I felt the fear.
I felt the anger.

And in all these things I got lost.
I lost my way.
And here I am.
Lost.
Seeking to find my way back home.

ABOUT MEDITATION

A light,
Shining in the depths of the universe,
Not controlled by fear,
Not controlled by anger,
Not controlled by desire,
Not controlled by emotions.

In command of my life,
A light shining in brilliance,
Embraced by joy,
Being ALL that I AM.

Happiness

Happiness is often a misunderstood concept or state of being. True happiness can only be understood after it is experienced. In other words, when one has lived and felt this happiness, then, and only then, comes the realization that it is something which cannot be defined with words. Describing it is as impossible as describing colour to the blind. Every individual is meant to exist in this state of true and undefinable happiness.

Lifetime upon lifetime of choices has led human society astray—away from this reality—so that the normal and natural state of existence was eventually lost and forgotten. "Normal" and "natural" in today's world include a variety of states which are often based on fear. For example, two such states of "unnatural" or false happiness are the accumulation of material possessions or being in a position of power where others can be controlled for personal gain. One might also mistake happiness as a hypnotic state of infatuation.

During the practice of meditation, a state can be achieved where the consciousness is expanded to embrace the Life Force. It is an elevated state filled with potential. It can open a doorway which will lead back to the natural state of true and undefinable happiness. Manifesting the lessons learnt from the practice will evolve into a journey from one's current state of being to a state which existed at the beginning of life. This journey and the states of existence will be described in more detail later.

On life's journey, happiness is the beginning and happiness is the end. There is no better time than now to start polishing the compass which points in the direction of happiness. It is a journey which starts the moment the choice is made to follow the compass and ends at the place where true happiness, in all its glory, is embraced. Embark on this journey and life will never be the same. It will be filled with the most amazing moments. The doorway to the mysteries of one's own life will open. Be prepared to be amazed, but also be prepared to face difficult challenges which can sometimes feel too great to be endured. Anticipate being in the state of true happiness, and this consequently will build the courage and strength to persevere through the hardships of the journey.

When looking back at the past, it is easy for the mind to be lulled into a state of stupor by dwelling on erroneous choices. One might fixate on the errors which have wounded the conscious mind, allowing precious happiness to bleed away. But such errors from the past do not change life forever, for the power to reverse course and return to the place of happiness lies within everyone.

Take heed of the Nazarene master's wisdom to *"Take up your bed and walk." (John 5:8, Holy Bible, King James Version)*. It is a metaphor for the return journey—one of healing. It is saying that blindness created by soporific patterns must end. It is time to rise above the slumberous state and take responsibility for past actions. It is time to end the patterns which energized devolution and assume the responsibility to correct them. (The process of devolution will be discussed in more detail later.)

Regardless of the current station in life, answers will emerge from the meditative state. Listen to the dialogue which comes from the heart, for it is the voice of Truth offered within the consciousness. Engage the healing power which Truth offers. Follow the path which this Truth offers, for it will lead to the most amazing joy and more.

On this journey, true happiness will feel like nourishment for the consciousness. Always choose happiness as the goal, for it is the birthright of every life and within reach.

Part Two
Attitude

The Approach

Personal attitudes shape the way one views, interacts with and responds to the world. They reflect one's inner nature and hold the power to define and redefine the psyche. The practice of meditation can reveal attitudes which impact the nature of the psyche. Attitudes held during meditation will impact the outcome by redefining the psyche, which will lead to rebuilding oneself as a new person.

Thus, the practice of meditation holds the power to change lives—your life. Changes can be positive and negative. Before starting to practice, it is therefore important to hold only positive attitudes. Thus, choose attitudes which are underlined by Love and Truth. For example:

> 1. *To understand who I am and how I may become all that I am meant to be.*

2. *To satisfy the needs of the body, mind, and Spirit.*

3. *To express humility in all interactions.*

4. *To be patient and kind to everyone.*

5. *To receive guidance for self and other seekers.*

6. *To become an instrument of Love and Truth.*

7. *To avoid the experience of despair or failure.*

8. *To protect oneself and other seekers, lest paths may falter.*

9. *To heal the mind and body and become a vessel of Love and Truth.*

10. *To become an instrument of the Life Force in the physical world.*

11. *To become a Light for those who seek or falter.*

12. *To be merciful to those who lack an understanding of Love and Truth.*

The Journey

The traditional meaning of meditation is "guided contemplation", however, it can be more than that. The practice evolves into a journey—one with a clear beginning and end. It starts when one decides to meditate and ends when the lessons offered during meditation are integrated in one's life. When learning to meditate, one of the first steps is developing an awareness of the mind and knowing when it is quiet. It is important to recognize when thoughts enter and how to address them.

The beginning of the journey is the current state of being. The end is the final objective; however as one meditates, the final objective can shift and change. It can change due to personal growth or because of changes in perceptions and awareness.

A basic understanding of the mind will aid in this journey. View the mind as an entity where thoughts enter and leave. Each thought has a basis and an objective. The nature of thoughts can be viewed as infinite in number since they continuously enter the mind. Some thoughts have greater power than others based on the attention they demand. Thoughts can emerge from recent, past, or hidden memories. Thoughts and memories are intimately tied to the senses. Hearing a song or experiencing a particular scent can awaken memories of past events or experiences. Emotions—such as anger, love, jealousy, etc.—associated with those events or experiences may emerge. The nature of the individual's psyche will determine how emotions are addressed. Becoming aware of how you respond to different emotions is an important step along the journey of learning to meditate.

The practice of meditation can be used to shape or direct an individual's response to thoughts. The process of thinking, and how a person responds to thoughts, are functions of the conscious mind. Functions which pertain to the intrinsic nature of the individual, such as free will, choice, courage, and power, also determine how one responds to thought. There are even deeper aspects which extend beyond the mind that are building blocks which form the foundation of the psyche. An individual's actions, choices, and responses to situations are determined by the nature of these building blocks. Meditation offers opportunities to disassemble the building blocks. An individual may choose materials such as Love and Truth to rebuild a new foundation.

Embarking on the journey which emerges from the practice of meditation is a personal choice one might make due to a desire to change or to embrace the essence of life. What is most important is honouring that choice. To honour a personal choice is simply honouring oneself. On the journey, distractions will appear. The mind likes to be busy. It likes to chatter about experiences, situations, hopes, desires, etc. The nature of the mind is to have fun. The mind likes to play games. The mind likes to be in control. The mind does not like change. Ultimately, the mind likes to feel safe. One must realize that one of the mind's basic natures is self-protection, which includes protecting the psyche. The mind resists commands to remain quiet when one tries to practice meditation. The mind views such commands as threats for two reasons: the potential that the psyche will change, and the loss of its control. The primary objective of the practice is change, so naturally the mind will resist. What is more threatening, however, is losing control to a force greater than the mind itself—the Life Force within, more commonly described as the Spirit.

When it's time to practice meditation, be prepared for shenanigans. The mind which will seek to kibosh the plans by finding other things to do, presenting them as more important. This is where real power comes into play. The free will to choose is far more powerful than the mind, as it is a function of the Spirit. It is important to remember this when preparing to meditate. Manifest that power from within and choose to honour the commitment made to yourself.

What Lies Beneath

The practice of meditation
opens doors to the inner self,
to reveal amazing truths.

Learn what lies beneath the surface
hidden from the sight of the conscious mind,
and realize it is part of who we are.

We may not feel ready
to see what lies beneath,
but in time we will
if we wish to embrace our totality
and find the happiness that totality offers.

Thus, take the time to meditate.

Learn about self,
and what life can offer.

Learn to meditate.
And discover the truths
about who we are.

Manifest truth
by embarking on a journey
where all that we are
is embraced.

Amen

Part Three
Preparation

The practice of meditation requires the skill of stilling the body and mind. In the same way that a musician must practice often to master a musical instrument, one's skill will improve with each meditation. With each session, it becomes easier to sit quietly for a desired period of time. It also becomes easier to quiet the mind. With regular practice, the experience becomes deeper, more satisfying, and more enjoyable. It becomes a time that is treasured. Preparation for the practice is as important as the act itself. There are three steps.

The **first step** is preparation of the environment. Choose a quiet room which will be undisturbed for a selected period of time. Dim, soothing lighting, scents, and relaxing music will enhance the environment. If the mind is even slightly concerned about the potential of being disturbed, the consciousness will not be able to find the state of calm. Ensuring the space will be undisturbed for the selected period of time will remove that concern.

Preparing the body is the **second step**, and equally important. During the practice, the body will object to sitting quietly. Muscles will complain, the skin will itch, and the back will hurt. Address these prior to meditating. Wearing a loose garment and cleansing oneself with pure water will help.

Twenty minutes of gentle walking in an environment with fresh air will relax the body. Alternatively, fifteen minutes of gentle and relaxing physical exercise will also help. This can include activities such as yoga, stretching, or flexing individual muscles.

Improving the energy flow along the spine will also be an aid. Gentle head and neck exercises will relieve strain in the area and open the energy channels between the base of the spine and the head. While doing these exercises, use the cleansing breath. Gently fill the lungs from the diaphragm all the way to the top and rapidly exhale by using the diaphragm to force the air swiftly through the nose. Then, use the cleansing breath three times after the exercise. The following head and neck exercises were given by *Edgar Cayce*.

"Sitting erect, bend the head forward three times, to the back three times, to the right side three times, to the left side three times, and then circle the head each way three

times. Don't hurry through with it but take the time to do it." (Edgar Cayce readings 3549-1).

The **third step** is choosing a posture. One of the most comfortable postures is sitting on a firm and solid chair with the feet placed flat on the floor. The chair should be deep enough to support the back in a comfortable erect position. Some may choose to sit on the floor cross-legged. Choose whatever posture works best for the body and the chosen amount of time. Whatever position is used, keep the legs slightly apart and the hands on the lap facing downward. If there is a desire and an inclination to clasp the hands, then do this initially until the position can be comfortably changed to the lap. The correct posture will enhance rather than restrict the energy flow of the Life Force within.

Part Four
Purpose

The word "purpose" can be defined as the "aim or goal of a person". For each human life, there is an ultimate purpose. Achieving this purpose often requires many steps. If enlightenment is one's ultimate purpose, then the practice of meditation can be one of the steps which can accelerate success.

The *Book of Ecclesiastes* was written about two thousand, five hundred years ago and contains the wisdom of King Solomon about the grand design of life. It includes words such as *"To everything there is a season, and a time to every purpose under heaven." (Ecclesiastes 1:1, Holy Bible, King James Version)*. This wisdom can be applied to all life here on Earth today. For example, the mighty oak tree sheds its acorns during the season of autumn. Buried deep within each seed lies a purpose, which becomes evident by the potential within its heart to take root and grow into a mighty oak tree. Nurtured by the sunlight and raindrops, this potential is made manifest and substantiated by the existence of oak forests around the world.

Humans likewise belong to the grand design of all life as outlined by King Solomon, each having a purpose which can be manifested in its season, when nurtured. This is the purpose which can be nurtured with the practice of meditation. However, fulfilling any purpose can require several steps. Like climbing a ladder to a rooftop where the view expands to encompass the horizon, each step expands the consciousness to ultimately arrive at the place of total enlightenment.

According to King Solomon in the *Book of Ecclesiastes*, the "season" for humans can be interpreted as a single lifetime. Arriving at the top of the ladder requires only a single lifetime. However, many lifetimes may be utilized to achieve this goal. Further insight may be found in the story of Jacob's Ladder *(Genesis 28:10-32, Holy Bible, King James Version)*.

The ultimate goal which emerges from the practice of meditation is achieving a state where the subconscious and the conscious minds unite as one. This is the state where enlightenment is achieved. It is the state when one arrives at the top of the proverbial ladder of life. However, on the path to total enlightenment, one must traverse each step of the ladder. Each rung on the ladder represents a stage of life, and meditation sessions will focus on aims and goals for that particular phase of one's life. Identifying the attitude to be held during the practice will define a path towards its fulfillment. When it is difficult to identify the current aim in life, simply framing the session with an attitude of expectancy underlined by Love and Truth will manifest clarity.

The practice of meditation can be used to understand the current stage in life. It can also be used as a source of guidance for fulfilling each successive aim, and for eventually arriving at the final aim or grand purpose of enlightenment.

An understanding of the mechanics involved in the evolution of personal aims will aid in traversing the ladder of life. Many meander through life aimlessly, living from day to day, consciously unaware of any purpose. They follow a pattern which was imprinted within their minds by parents or society. In so doing, personal wishes are being denied without consciously realizing that it is happening.

There is, however, a subconscious purpose which is based on a path that was established by personal choices—choices which emerged from emotional, mental, and physical challenges along life's journey. These are the choices which define life as it is in the moment. These are the choices which have created the current framework. Successive choice throughout life can be viewed as a pathway that leads to the current station in life. When traced backwards, it would lead to a previous state of being or framework. This may be the mental framework of the person as a child. It may also lead to a framework from a previous life. Ultimately, it will lead to the framework or state of being which existed within the mind during the first lifetime here on earth. What an amazing thought!

All the stages of the path travelled can be revealed during the practice of meditation.

Seekers of this path may originate from different walks of life. Some feel compelled to seek answers about the nature and purpose of life immediately after surviving a personal tragedy. Similarly, a traumatic experience can cause a change in focus and fill the mind with questions. Others may naturally be seekers. The crucial element, however, is conscious awareness of unanswered questions and a quest for answers. How the questions are addressed has the potential to change the trajectory of life or define a new path forward. These are the questions to hold within the mind during meditation.

During the practice of meditation, an elevated state can be achieved where the conscious and subconscious unite as one to reveal current and past memories and emotions that are impacting life today. In this elevated state, meditation holds the potential to offer new perspectives on life. It also serves as a source of wisdom to make different choices. When faced again with similar emotional, mental, and physical challenges, these new choices offer the opportunity to change the trajectory of life.

The practice of meditation expands the consciousness to a place where life is scrutinized in every detail. It is the opportunity to look at oneself objectively. It is an opportunity to dissect and disassemble the consciousness and understand the subconscious self. It offers the opportunity to reassemble and rebuild the self on a different foundation—upon the metaphoric rock of eternal Truth held together by the mortar of eternal Love. This is the purpose to be realized and then ultimately embraced when practicing the art of meditation.

In essence, the purpose for being here at this time and place is to embrace the opportunity to change. Growth is only possible with change. The purpose of life can be defined as growing towards the totality of self, which is the mental framework that existed in the beginning, during the first lifetime here on Earth. It is about returning to that original state of being that existed before the journey of choice began. Restoring that initial state, where the mind was framed with enlightenment, is the ultimate purpose and state of being to be achieved during the journey which emerges from the practice of meditation. It was a state of being where one was able to say with conviction, as God said to Moses, *"I AM WHO I AM" (Exodus 3:14, Holy Bible, King James Version).*

Part Five
Duality

We can all agree the freedom to choose is a foundational element of human life. Whenever there are two or more possibilities, this freedom can be exercised. It is estimated that, on the average, a choice is made in every two seconds of a person's life. Thus, a billion or more choices would be made in each lifetime. These choices lead to a dual nature in human existence. It is built into the psyche of everyone and frames every situation whenever a choice is to be made. Duality becomes apparent when multiple possibilities create internal conflict during the decision-making process. An understanding of the nature of duality will aid in the process of decision-making. Meditation, when practiced with a level of dedication, will bring forth a certain type of clarity which would offer objectivity to the dynamics of choosing. The metaphorical ladder of life (discussed in the previous chapter) is bidirectional. The consciousness can evolve or devolve based on the nature of a choice. Certain choices will lead upwards while others will lead downwards. The evolution or expansion of the consciousness is symbolized by an upward movement on the ladder, while a downward movement symbolizes contraction or devolution.

Whenever a decision is to be made, an inner voice can be heard speaking quietly from somewhere within the deep recesses of the mind. A closer look will reveal threads connecting the decision to a current aim in life. The physical, mental, emotional, and spiritual aspects of the decision are being assessed. The nature of the person's psyche will determine whether internal conflict will arise between the possibilities that are being considered.

The inner voice could relate to any current or anticipated situation, such as pursuing education, finding a suitable job, acquiring wealth, achieving health and longevity, improving physical beauty, visiting far-away places, finding a soul mate, or even the meaning of life. Feelings connected to the psyche are associated with the inner voice. These feelings fall in two categories. They are either seeded with fear, or with Love. A choice based on Love leads in one direction on the ladder of life, while one based on fear will lead in a different direction. These define two very different pathways that illustrate the dual nature of life.

The dual nature of life guides us to better understand the functioning of the consciousness. The consciousness is a window into the psyche. The psyche, in turn, is a window into the Life Force. Love is the underlying nature of the Life Force and forms the building blocks of the psyche. Fear also holds a place within the dynamics of the psyche. Together, these are responsible for the creation of consciousness and its dual nature.

Although these dynamics apply to everyone, there are some who do not face the challenges of duality. Living a life underlined only by Love, one holds the power to transcend the reaches of duality.

The practice of meditation holds the potential to bring objectivity to any situation. A dedicated practice will open the door to the Life Force, which will inject awareness within the consciousness about the nature of the situation and its options. Connected to this awareness are feelings which denote whether a choice is seeded by Love or fear.

These are the feelings which can be used to determine a direction on the ladder of life. Choices based on Love (which flow from the Life Force) will navigate life upwards towards an enlightened consciousness. It is the path of evolution. The converse is also true. Choices seeded by fear will navigate a path of devolution. These two opposing paths within the consciousness illustrate the dual nature of existence.

ABOUT MEDITATION

When starting to meditate for the first time, challenges will be encountered. Finding difficulty in achieving the state of objectivity is quite normal. If this occurs, it is an indication that the momentum of one's current trajectory in life holds power over the psyche. Deeper meditation through perseverance is required to transcend this momentum. Being grounded by the knowledge that only one lifetime is required to achieve enlightenment will help with the practice.

Choices that are underlined by Love can be viewed as building blocks that expand the consciousness. The objective awareness of personal feelings (wants or desires) offers an opportunity to exercise the free will to choose. The response by the Life Force will be unique for each person, predicated by their history (traditions, economics, and social norms). Meditation offers the objectivity to transcend all aspects of a person's life, including the patterns established by their history, changing the trajectory.

Consider an example where someone wants to feel powerful. Perhaps it is a parent who seeks respect from their children or someone who wants to be controlling in a relationship. It could also be a boss who bullies, a CEO of a huge corporation who demands results, or a prime minister or president who wants power over the lives of the people. Regardless of who you are, exercising free will is required in order to fulfill such desires. Typically, the mind will see two options. Either embrace the path which offers power, or find another way. On the surface, for each of these individuals, choosing would seem a simple process. However, the practice of meditation can be used to transcend any trajectory created by historical ties, enabling an objective choice.

Choosing may be complicated further by karmic history—the journey of experiences which brought the person to the present situation. Deep emotions connected to past experiences can make it difficult to find objectivity. For example, the psyche of a person who abused power will result in consciousness filled with guilt, regret, and shame. The memory of such experiences is available to the Life Force throughout eternity. For most, the memory of the events would be vague shadows. However, the connected emotions such as guilt, regret, and shame would resurface when similar situations occur.

In this example, the person has the freedom to walk away, forgoing the opportunity to face a similar outcome from the past, thereby not allowing fear to dictate their trajectory in life. Due to the karmic connection, the person would also have an innate awareness of the potential the situation offers—to revisit a situation and relive the deep emotions. Following an old pattern etched in the psyche by past experience will feel easy and natural. The draw of etched patterns will be strong. The dual nature of the psyche is illustrated by the desire to either walk away or to relive the emotions of the past.

With the strength, courage, wisdom, and objectivity offered by the practice of meditation, a person could choose to manifest only Love and Truth, thereby transcending the events of the past. In the case of the parent, only acceptance based on Love would manifest. The boss or CEO would manage with fairness. The prime minister or president would lead with Love, compassion, and justice. All of these actions would transcend the events of the past, forging a new trajectory in life. This is a path of growth through change and movement upward on the ladder of life.

The foundation of duality posits there are always two choices, directions, or pathways. One path leads back to the original state of existence, while the other continues, unchanged, along the current trajectory. The dual nature of life is always present. By mastering the practice of meditation, the objectivity that it offers will become a compass pointing to the original state of existence where the journey of life started, the place of enlightenment. It is up to each individual to embrace the power to choose a direction.

Part Six
Stillness

"And he arose, and rebuked the wind, and said unto the sea, Peace, be still. And the wind ceased, and there was a great calm." (Mark 4:39, Holy Bible, King James Version).

The human body is still when it is devoid of motion. Abstaining from physical motion is one of the challenges faced during the practice of meditation. While the body may be silent, thoughts can flow through the mind like dry leaves tossed about on a tempestuous sea. Calming the mind to the point where the water is still and the leaves are stationary may be a greater challenge. With practice, the mind can be commanded to "be still".

The brain can be viewed as a very complicated computer that manages the physical body and its relationship with the surrounding environment. The mind can be viewed as the intelligent programming that operates the computer (brain). It does so by interfacing with the psyche, consciousness, and Life Force using the physical senses, feelings, perception, thoughts, will, and reason. The psyche is part of the Life Force that interfaces with the mind to access the consciousness. Thoughts flow from the mind to the consciousness to create awareness.

When the body is still, the mind is released from some of its tasks. When the body and mind are still, a doorway to the psyche opens, expanding the consciousness to include past memories and feelings from the Life Force. The practice of meditation requires both—stillness in body and mind. Thus, an important aspect of the practice is mastering the state of being still.

The consciousness is like the display screen of the mind. The screen becomes dim or blank during the state of stillness that occurs during the practice of meditation. When this happens, the mind is essentially inactive and its connection to the body and the physical environment is temporarily halted. This opens a doorway between the Life Force and the consciousness. In deep meditative states, data flows through the door, activating the screen of the consciousness. Before the door closes, it is important to transfer this information to the conscious memory. Failing to do this means the experience will be forgotten. Mentally reviewing the information before stirring the body will transfer it to the conscious memory. At the end of the session, this information is now accessible by the mind.

Recording the events in a journal will further preserve the memory for later analysis. The mind can use the information during the objective process of decision making.

There are **three stages** in achieving the state of stillness. First, stillness of the body, then the mind, and finally the consciousness. All are required in order to enter into the meditative state.

The **first stage** is stilling the body. This requires patience. It also requires an attitude of inner calm in order to maintain a chosen posture for the selected period of time. During this exercise, keep in mind the heart pumps blood to the lungs where it is oxygenated with the breath and distributed through the arteries to the rest of the body. Improving the flow of oxygen can be achieved by calming the body with breathing exercises. Inhale deeply and calmly then slowly exhale. The following breathing exercises were given by *Edgar Cayce.*

"Breathe in through the right nostril three times, and exhale through the mouth. Breathe in three times through the left nostril and exhale through the right." (Edgar Cayce reading 281-13).

This will calm the respiratory system while improving circulation throughout the body. The calm will be an aid in stilling the body.

Following the breathing exercises, place the hands in the position chosen for meditating and gently relax. Then, mentally focus the consciousness on the body, starting from the sole of the feet and slowly progressing to the crown of the head. Methodically, focus on each part of the body with a mental instruction to relax all the muscles associated with the area. As each instruction is issued, patiently and calmly wait for the sensation of relaxation to be felt, then progress upwards to the next area. Once this is completed, the entire body will feel extremely calm and relaxed.

The **second stage** is stilling the mind. Calming certain glands within the body will help sustain the state of stillness. This is done by listening to the pulse of the heart while focusing on the area of glands within the body in a specific order: gonads, lyden, pancreas, thymus, thyroid, pineal, and pituitary. As each gland is brought into focus, visualize a colour in each area, in the following order: red, orange, yellow, green blue, indigo, and purple. These correspond to the chakras in the following order: root, sacral, solar plexus, heart, throat, third eye, and crown. The chakra system is based on Hindu philosophy as outlined in the Upanishads (author unknown.) These steps hold the potential to restore the natural function of the glands, a precursor to the state of calm.

Start this process by listening for a heartbeat. Do this by focusing the mind on the area of the heart. Feel the pulse like a gentle rhythm within the calmed aura of the body. Focus on this pulse. Slowly and gently inhale, then relax further with each exhalation. With each breath, focus on the glands, starting at the root and proceeding sequentially to the crown. At the end of the process, the body and the mind will be still. With practice, one would be able to simply command the mind to "be still".

The **third stage** involves using the mind to still the consciousness. Take the focus of the mind outside the body. Become aware of the chair or the floor where you are sitting. Expand the awareness of the calm body to include the floor, walls, and then the ceiling of the room. Continue to expand the awareness to include the building. Go beyond the building to include the area surrounding the building. Include the streets, parks, and other structures. Include the whole town or city, then the whole country. Expand the awareness to include the oceans, continents, islands, and then the whole world. Expand the consciousness beyond the earth to include the planets of the solar system. Visualize the planets rotating around the sun and the earth below in its blue magnificence. Include the sun and the stars far beyond. Travel among the stars to the depth of the cosmos and fill the consciousness with all that exists.

At this stage, the mind will be silent and the conscious devoid of thoughts and, as a result, receptive.

Within the silence, there will be a feeling of deep peacefulness. Within this peacefulness, be vigilant, as thoughts will wander in. When this happens, be patient. Take a moment to analyze the thought. There will be two types, based on the source. Thoughts will originate from either the mind or the Life Force. The mind may repeat thoughts from current situations. Honour them. Ask them to wait for a more conducive time and bid them farewell.

Within the state of stillness, be patient. Embrace an attitude of expectancy. Keep calm and wait for the emergence of the Life Force. While waiting, follow the breath as it enters the body all the way down to the diaphragm. Then follow the breath as it leaves the body, from the diaphragm all the way through the nostrils. Between each breath, listen to the beat of the heart. Continue these exercises for the remaining time set aside or until the presence of the Life Force is felt within the consciousness.

Within the state of stillness, be patient. In the *Gospel of John*, the Nazarene Master speaks of patiently holding an attitude of expectancy while waiting for the emergence of the Life Force within the consciousness.

"And I will pray the Father, and he shall give you another Comforter, that he may abide with you for ever; Even the Spirit of truth; whom the world cannot receive, because it seeth him not, neither knoweth him: but ye know him; for he dwelleth with you, and shall be in you. I will not leave you comfortless: I will come to you." (John 14:16-18, Holy Bible, King James Version).

Another notable biblical reference comes from Luke, where he writes in the *Book of Acts* about the types of experiences one may encounter.

"And suddenly there came a sound from heaven as of a rushing mighty wind, and it filled all the house where they were sitting. And there appeared unto them cloven tongues like as of fire, and it sat upon each of them. And they were all filled with the Holy Ghost, and began to speak with other tongues, as the Spirit gave them utterance." (Acts 2:2-4, Holy Bible, King James Version).

Part Seven
The Embracing Life Force

Each person's life as a human being is a delicate balance between cells from the earth and the Life Force. The process starts at conception as cells are gathered together around the Life Force to form a human body. Nourished by the earth, the body grows to adulthood, ages, and then the cells return to the earth upon physical death, releasing its connection with the Life Force. The course of a lifetime is filled with choices and experiences which influence the direction of the person's life. These choices have a direct connection with the equilibrium between the cells (the human body) and the embracing Life Force. As described in the chapter on Duality, this balance can be disturbed by choices which are not in harmony with the Life Force.

The Life Force is commonly known as the Spirit. It is the source of creative expression within existence. Its awareness encompasses the psyche, consciousness (mind), unconsciousness (psyche) and all that exists. Each physical life is an expression of a Life Force.

The energies emitted by the Life Force are a form of Love and Truth. These are elements of reality which can be described as Spiritual Love (Part Eleven) and Spiritual Truth (Part Twelve). Unlike the love and truth described in traditional dictionaries, which are connected to the mind and relate to a different physical energy, these are connected directly to the Life Force. The Love and Truth described in this book pertain to the Life Force or Spirit and are capitalized.

The psyche was originally a perfect reflection of the Life Force. It harmonized with the mind to create the consciousness or the awareness of a human being. Life was in perfect balance. Through time, the application of choice changed the nature of the mind. This change reflected back into the psyche and, as a result, it no longer represented the image of the Life Force. The balance was disturbed. The psyche, in combination with the mind, formed a unit called the soul. Thus, a soul is created in each physical lifetime.

The brain can be viewed as a computer that manages the physical body and its relationship with the surrounding environment.

The mind can be viewed as the intelligent programming that operates the computer. It does so by interfacing with the psyche, consciousness, and Life Force, using the physical senses, feelings, perception, thoughts, will, and reason.

The consciousness is awareness of the physical and non-physical elements created by the psyche through the mind.

Reality can be viewed as existence within realms. Realms are also described as dimensions or vibratory levels. Physical life exists in a three-dimensional realm, which can be perceived with the human senses. The Life Force, on the other hand, cannot be seen with the naked eye or felt with human senses, as it exists in a different realm. One can become aware of its presence during the state of stillness, which occurs when practicing meditation. It is the same with the psyche, mind, and consciousness. They all exist in realms outside the reach of the human senses, similar to the Life Force. One can become aware of their existence and their roles in the unfolding of life here on Earth during the state of silence. The experience of human life is the result of a temporal multidimensional construct of the Life Force, psyche, mind, and consciousness.

Souls are attached to the Spirit or Life Force by threads commonly known as karma. By dissolving these threads through the spiritualization of the mind, the associated parts of the psyche are restored to their original states and re-merge with the Life Force.

Spiritualization of the mind can occur by making choices which are in harmony with the Life Force. Whenever a choice is made, it holds the potential to re-engineer the mind by replacing its old patterns with new ones. The process of spiritualizing occurs when the patterns are in harmony with the Life Force or Spirit.

Karma is an imprint on the psyche resulting from choices made during a lifetime. The psyche lives on beyond physical death, and it can become part of a future incarnation here on the earth. The patterns imprinted within the psyche will remain in the background until they can be applied to new situations. When this happens, it is an opportunity to dissolve the karma by making choices that harmonize with the Life Force.

Prayer is appealing to the mind, consciousness, psyche, soul, and Life Force. The framework of prayer is creating an attitude of expectancy.

The practice of meditation is the process of listening inwardly for answers. The focus of the practice is the creation of a state of silence where answers emerge.

The state of balance is achieved when the energy of the Life Force is being transmitted without alteration or filters through each of the energy centers of the physical body.

The light which illuminates from within is the energy that is emitted from the Life Force and is composed of Love and Truth. It is also known as Divine Light.

The Life Force, also known as the Spirit, is the force or energy responsible for animating physical life here on Earth.

Faith is acceptance of the non-evidential existence of an indwelling Life Force or Spirit which is responsible for animating the physical body. Applying faith is using the inner guidance which emerges from the Life Force in conjunction with free will for self-determination.

In order to revisit choices from the past which resulted in karma and to spiritualize the mind by making different choices, one must first have the ability to recognize the presence of the Life Force when it is active within the consciousness. One of the objectives of practicing meditation is gaining this ability. It occurs during the state of stillness. This ability can be used to recognize when the Love and Truth can be applied in a situation. The application of Love and Truth will restore balance.

During the practice, the consciousness, which was created by the mind and psyche, becomes still. This occurs when the filters, which created the perception of life, become silent. For example, filters such as love for a spouse, anger towards a neighbour, jealousy toward colleagues, fear of losing a job or providing food and housing for a family, disappointing a friend, or desire for wealth, are just a few of the elements which are responsible for the nature of the consciousness. When all the filters are silenced, the only presence within the consciousness is the Love and Truth flowing from the Life Force. When this occurs, within the stillness one may see visions, experience healing or have profound feelings. These are opportunities to look at one's life objectively.

For some, it may feel like wearing new glasses, offering a perception of life that is clearer and crisper. It allows situations to be viewed through the spectacles of Love and Truth, offering different perspectives. If this occurs, be prepared to face this whirlwind of new feelings. Suitability of existing relationships, jobs, places to live, etc., will be questioned. Past issues that once held importance will no longer be a motivating force in life. Everything in life will be questioned.

This new awareness is the true nature of life, which was hidden like a lamp under a bushel basket. *(The lamp under the bushel basket analogy was given by the Nazarene master in Matthew 5:15, Holy Bible, King James Version.)* Like turning on an electric light in a darkened room, removing the bushel basket symbolizes a new form of clarity offered by the practice of meditation.

At the end of each practice, take a moment to recall the sensations that were experienced. Describe all the details in a journal with the expectation of recognizing situations where change can be applied while outside the meditative state. One of the objectives of the practice is gaining the ability to consciously use the Life Force as a guide when making all choices, thereby spiritualizing the mind, and consequently, the psyche and consciousness. With dedication to the practice, all of life's experiences will begin to resonate with the Life Force. All of life will become one with Love and Truth, creating a path which will lead to the top of the ladder of life (Part Four).

Part Eight
Follow Me

Many of the messages offered by the *Holy Bible* can be interpreted like dreams. The symbolism is so powerful, it can even be applied to life today. The phrase "Follow Me" appears in several places. For example, the Nazarene master shared, *"Whosoever will come after me, let him deny himself, and take up his cross, and follow me." (Mark 8:34, Holy Bible, King James Version)*. In another notable occurrence, the writer said, *"And as Jesus passed forth from thence, he saw a man, named Matthew, sitting at the receipt of custom: and he saith unto him, Follow me. And he arose, and followed him." (Matthew 9:9, Holy Bible, King James Version)*.

When searching for answers, the practice of meditation may not be the only avenue. The *Holy Bible* is only one example of timeless wisdom which can be tapped into, if one is willing to look beyond mainstream interpretations and misinterpretations. This simple phrase "Follow Me" speaks of internal guidance. However, guidance can also originate from external sources.

For example, "let him deny himself" or "take up his cross" both speak of challenges in personal life. The first phrase speaks of transcending the ego. In the second phrase, the Nazarene master speaks of dissolving karma. The example from the *Gospel of Matthew* can be a little frightening. If guided by the Life Force, one must be prepared to walk away from any life situation without hesitation. It can be frightening because it could mean leaving a lucrative job or separating from family or friends. As a natural course, all of life's challenges will be faced with hurdles. Doubt is often a tactic created by the mind and the cornerstone of failure. For example, "How will I support myself without a job?" or "Will I be happy without friends or a spouse?" The phrase "Follow Me", when offered by the Life Force, means moving towards a life that is conducive to the path of enlightenment.

External sources relate to social patterns where there is an implied expectation of conformity. In times gone by, religion was a good example within western society where dogma was preached and blindly followed by many. The inquiring nature of modern society has largely transcended this form of lifestyle, but in the east, religion still plays a huge role in the direction of lives. There are many cases where physical lives were blindly sacrificed by following misinterpreted scripture. It is a case where social patterns have overshadowed the Life Force to become the voice which was followed.

The practice of meditation can be used to embrace objectivity and tap into the inner source of guidance founded upon the facets of the Life Force, which are Love and Truth. The practice can be used to identify whether guidance is coming from an internal or external source. Whether from the east or west, one must willingly choose the gentle voice of the Life Force appealing to the consciousness to "Follow Me."

Part Nine
The Inner Voice

The LORD came and stood there, calling as at the other times, "Samuel! Samuel!" Then Samuel said, "Speak, for your servant is listening." (1 Samuel 3:10, The Holy Bible, King James Version).

The true nature of life is easily forgotten and reality becomes an illusion which evolves from challenges and experiences that occur while navigating the avenues of polarizing thought within society. Agendas of individuals, factions, and groupings are pulling people in all directions. It is easy to become lost in the struggles between factions, resulting in changing focus and purpose. Choosing a path of detachment does not insulate the mind from these ways of the world unless it involves total isolation, such as a life of navel gazing in a cave in the Himalayas. This reality of the world today is influencing the direction life is taking on the planet.

Step back for a moment of introspection and observe that life is the result of a collection of cells animated by a Life Force. A simple disturbance within the group of cells would interrupt the ability of the Life Force to have full expression. Disturbances could result from changing environmental conditions such as climate change, something more intrusive like an automobile accident, or even the unexplainable such as cancers or organ failure. Life continues onward on the planet, notwithstanding the veil of these potentialities that impact each individual.

Reality is based on the perception which emerges from the physical senses. Life therefore is a combination of cells animated by a Life Force based on input from physical senses. The physical senses respond to waves of thought generated by society. This defines the nature of human existence. In essence, it is an illusion which originated from the beginning of life on the planet.

The *Book of Genesis* in the *Holy Bible* illustrates the evolution of the mind using an example where two people succumb to temptation. In today's world, moral and ethical acceptability are evolving concepts and are no longer based on the fundamentals of Love and Truth, as it was in the beginning. A close look will reveal the factors which eroded the fundamental nature of life, such as the desire for power to control for the purpose of profit. The world today is simply based on these two factors—control and profit. The minds of individuals have been systematically engineered to be part of this system. Everything about the true and pure nature of life is being forgotten because of the types of illusions held within the minds of individuals.

Many would argue that they are not impacted, and it is true that some are not. However, it impacts everyone who is involved in the social and economic systems which are part of today's existence.

In an ideal world, money should be a representation of people's time. However, within the system of today's economy, the word "interest" has infused everyone's lives, tainting the concept of the ethics of fairness. It has been accepted as part of a system in society, blindly ignoring that it was created using control and greed. This is part of the illusion held within the mind as "reality".

Everything about the true nature of life is forgotten because life has become so busy with all the activities of this world. Day after day, new concepts are introduced, marketed and easily accepted as part of the new way of life. There is nothing wrong with building and creating, provided it is all based on the nature of existence, which is Love and Truth. However, a close look would often reveal something different, something that is evolving out of the desire for control or greed. Within this frenzy of change, a trajectory based on a false nature is perpetuated moment after moment and day after day.

Again, there is nothing wrong with change. The basics of life are dependent on change. In order to grow, change must be embraced. However, only certain kinds of change result in growth. Growth is dependent on disassembling errors created by past choices that were based on a false nature. Many facets of the modern world crept into existence and built a life based on a false foundation, one which was not founded upon Love and Truth. This changed everything. It is now necessary to find ways to refocus on Love and Truth despite a reality where the illusion of existence is based on errors.

Each perception of reality is created out of an illusion based on the mechanics and architectural design of life. In each moment, choice determines the trajectory of the reality being created, and if errors will emerge when Love and Truth are ignored. As illustrated in the *Book of Genesis*, temptation is a force with the power to change the trajectory of life.

It is easily forgotten that the human body is made of countless cells that have come together to serve at the pleasure of a Life Force which embraces it. Life here on Earth is for the enjoyment of the physical realm, and this is possible by embracing the principles of existence and creation, which are Love and Truth. The architectural design and mechanics of the body must operate in precision for the consciousness to experience all the aspects of life here on Earth. When these enabling factors are ignored, life instead follows a trajectory that emerges out of temptation and based on patterns such as the economy, environment or religion.

It sounds complicated, but yet so simple. It is the simple things which were ignored that created the nature of life as it exists here on Earth today. Meditation holds the power to awaken this realization and change the trajectory of each individual that is willing to chart a new course, one based on the true nature of existence, one simply based on Love and Truth. Learning to meditate is learning the art of listening to oneself and realizing that there are choices which can impact the trajectory of life.

Each human being evolved from a place of unimaginable wisdom. Meditation is the art of opening to channel this wisdom from deep within the consciousness. One can choose to manifest this wisdom.

Samuel

There is a force within which seeks command.
It brings fear when one does not want to be afraid.
It manifests sickness when one would rather be well.
There is no freedom from this force.
It is always peering down over life.
It knows everything.
It sees everything.
It holds the power to control all of life.
During meditation, whom shall I seek?
It is the commanding force of life from within.
It is the voice which called to Samuel.
How shall I respond!
"Speak, for your servant is listening."
(1 Samuel 3:10, Holy Bible, King James Version)

Guidance emerges from within as a gentle voice appealing to the consciousness. Meditation will open this door. The Light which shines from within shares Love and Truth.

Part Ten
Dreams

Expect a whirlwind of changes in life when meditation is practiced regularly. For example, dreams may be initiated by the Life Force as a new source of guidance.

What the mind perceives as real are illusions derived from the sensory receptors of the physical body, interpreted and reflected onto the consciousness. The human response is based on wisdom derived from experiences, learnt behaviours, and conditioning from external sources. Outside this realm of human perceptions is a different reality, one created by the Life Force and not subject to time. It is a place which exists beyond the boundaries of physical reality as described in the chapter on the Life Force. From the perspective of the Life Force, it is the "true reality" and everything the physical body perceives through its senses as solid is the illusion.

Dreams fall into the category of "true reality". This may initially be confusing since it is outside the boundaries of traditional thought. The mind will struggle and attempt to stay within the confines of science and logic. Denial of any other existence is a normal reaction. Transcending denial requires faith in the unverifiable. It requires faith in the existence of the Life Force to transcend denial by the mind and apply objectivity to new, different, and non-traditional thought. Dreams will open a window into a different reality.

Dreams can be viewed as a language used by the Life Force for communication with the person's consciousness. In dreams, images from life experiences become symbolic. They are combined with emotions to create scenarios containing a message. Life experiences are unique to each person; thus, the language of dreams will also be unique.

Emotions felt in the dream state are real. The Life Force transmits the emotions into the mind, which creates a reaction in the consciousness. The dreamer may feel fear, love, peace, pain, anger, or hunger, amongst other emotions. The physical body responds to these emotions. For example, fear may cause the body to convulse or tremble. If the dream images include a physical attack, the body may experience sensations of the struggle such as an urge to escape, argue, or fight back. Upon awakening, the dreamer may not only remember the struggle, but also the feelings associated with it. The dream's message offers an objective perspective of a waking situation. This will allow the dreamer an opportunity to make different choices and navigate life in a new direction, perhaps away from a dangerous situation such as an oppressive boss, abusive spouse, etc.

Images, scenarios, and emotions offered in dreams typically emerge from past experiences. The practice of meditation can be utilized to examine and understand the dream. The message can be found by looking for parallels between the emotions triggered by the dream and those felt in a current life situation. Dreams which are ignored will reoccur, offering the message from different perspectives. Dreams can become nightmares if important messages continue to be ignored. Once the message is received and acted upon, the dreams will change or cease to occur.

The language of dreams is a tool for communicating between the Life Force and the consciousness. Learning to interpret dreams is an art which improves with practice. Confidence will grow once an interpretation is validated. Validation leads to a way of life where the guidance offered from dreams becomes integral to the way of life.

The practice of meditation holds the potential to induce dreams during sleep. Dreams may also occur while meditating and are viewed as visions. The process of interpretation is the same for both sources. New choices that emerge from the interpretation offer the opportunity to change one's trajectory in life.

When the dream world is honoured by following steps to remember, interpret, and integrate, the connection between the dream world and the physical world will grow stronger until they merge. Using dreams as guidance will become a powerful force in everyday living here on Earth.

Sleep

Eyes heavy with sleep,
The mind closes its eyes,
But the subconscious is always awake,
Alert and observing.

In a moment,
The consciousness stirs and gathers thought.
It nudges the mind into semi-sleep,
Scattering the thoughts before its sleepy eyes
That they may be glimpsed.

Then the mind is lulled back to sleep.
Nothingness.

What happened last night.
Was it a dream?
I wonder what it could mean.

The Cosmos

Journey into the cosmos,
Up and up away from the earth.
And like the view from the mountaintop
Where a vast landscape tantalizes the eyes,
From the depths of space
The vast cosmos-scape in its sparking glory
Would amaze the mind.

Embraced within the bosom of peace
By the deafening silence of the darkness,
A glorious sight to behold
Spots of light sprinkled everywhere,
Glistening like diamonds
As far as the consciousness could encompass.

But the experience defies logic,
So, the mind interferes
Causing the body to stir.
And consciousness returns
To the confines of the physical body
Which it inhabits.

Part Eleven
Love

The practice of meditation opens the door to aspects of life which have always existed but remained quietly operating in the background. During the state of stillness, when the Life Force emerges from the background, the awareness of Love and Truth is felt within the consciousness. It is notable that the natures of Love and Truth are different from what is traditionally known. The Love which emerges from the Life Force is the subject of this section. (Truth will be discussed later.)

It is said that "Love is the blood of the Spirit". This analogy was given to me by a Choctaw Shaman from the USA. Although all is connected, the Shaman looks at the mechanics of life from a non-physical perspective first. The Spirit (or Life Force) is responsible for the creation of each human life and Love is the underlying energy which makes it possible.

Traditionally, "love" is viewed from a physical perspective. Phrases such as "feelings towards another person" or a "romantic attraction towards another" are commonly used. This form of love applies to a connection with another person or an attachment to someone else. Physical items such as automobiles, houses, land, or money can also be the object of this form of "love".

The energy associated with traditional "love" relates to the physical aspects of life. It is activated by the sensory receptors within the body such as the eyes, tongue, nose, ears, and skin. The electrical charge generated by the receptors stimulate glands of the endocrine, releasing hormones into the bloodstream, resulting in urges. The mind then processes these urges in conjunction with karmic influences to create a reaction. Infatuation may be the result.

The Choctaw Shaman explained that the Love which flows from the Life Force is part of the structure of our being, much like blood which circulates through the body carrying life-giving oxygen to the cells of the physical structure. The energy circulates between the Life Force, psyche, mind, consciousness, and the chakras.

A mental image of this multidimensional construct can be viewed as multiple layers of energy encapsulating the physical body. The **first layer** is the brilliant energy of the Life Force. The **second layer** is the energy of the psyche. The **third layer** is the mind, and the consciousness is the **fourth**. The details of seven layers are tabulated in *Appendix A*. All the layers have their unique energy signatures. The colours emitted would be dependent on the nature of the person. Kirlian photography (invented in 1939 by Semyon Davidovitch Kirlian) detected a blue aura for someone engaged in the pursuit of Truth. Love added green to the aura. A white aura was detected if someone was living a totally balanced life. In most cases, all colours of the rainbow radiated around the physical body.

The chakras lie in a region between consciousness and the physical body. The endocrine system is the physical representation of the chakras and the interface between the non-physical and the physical. In the state of stillness created during the practice of meditation, the energy of Love flows unimpeded through the multidimensional circulatory system, activating all the chakras and their corresponding endocrine glands. This process can be paralleled with the calming of the respiration as discussed in Part Six, where breathing exercises are used to improve circulation and still the physical body.

Activation of the endocrine glands results in urges. For example, the thymus gland, which corresponds to the heart chakra, is the center of Love. A feeling of unconditional acceptance would fill the consciousness. The mind would process this feeling in conjunction with karmic influences and choose how to respond. For example, Love would balance the desire for abundance with charity.

Similarly, as each gland of the endocrine is energized, urges would emerge. Physical survivability is connected to the **root chakra** and the gonads. Pleasure is associated with the **sacral chakra** or the lyden gland. The power of the will is connected to the **solar plexus chakra** or the adrenal gland. As noted above, Love is connected to the **heart chakra** and the thymus gland. Truth is associated with the **throat chakra** or the thyroid gland. Insight is related to the **third eye chakra** or the pineal gland. The **crown chakra** is the center of enlightenment and connected to the pituitary gland in the center of the brain. These are also tabulated in *Appendix A*.

The dual nature of existence is reflected with the activation of the chakras. As noted, the mind would process the feelings in conjunction with karmic influence and choose how to respond. What is important to note is that the energy of Love is always present. All urges can be filtered by the heart chakra, applying unconditional acceptance. In other words, all impulses and inclinations can be directed through the heart chakra and the thymus to be tempered by the energy of Love or, according to the shaman, energized by "the blood of the spirit".

The Paradigm of Love

Love is not a game nor a word nor just a feeling.
It is a system within which we operate.

Love is the connection we have with each other,
whether friend, family, or foe.

Love is a paradigm as life is a paradigm.
The energy or the blood of that system is love.

We may say we hate someone, but they are a part of us.
We may feel we are unique, but we are all connected.
We are all made of the same material, carbon matter, or
cells from the earth.

We eat the same food and drink the same water.
Our lives depend on the same matter or food and air and
sunshine.
We all walk on the same Earth.

It is the paradigm of life.
The paradigm of love is what unites us or connects us.
When we smile at someone, they feel the connection.
That is the paradigm of love.

When we go to work and become part of a system
or part of an industry, the system or the industry is
connected by love.
And so, it is and so on.

Love is the Life Force or the blood of this world.
We can make it stronger by participating,

ABOUT MEDITATION

using wisdom and our inner guidance.
Then love will grow.
And
Happiness will grow.
Amen.

Part Twelve
Truth

The Nazarene master was asked "What is Truth?" *(The Gospel of John 18:38, Holy Bible, King James Version).* The question was not answered. Today, this question is still debated as many wonder what wisdom He would have offered. Traditionally, "truth" is viewed from a physical perspective and described as "a verifiable body of things, events, and facts". It relates to the physical word. Physical existence, however, is only part of the multidimensional construct of life. Understanding the nature and fabric of reality is an important step in understanding who we are and the role Truth plays in our lives.

Imagine the human body started from a single cell which grew from energy that came from the earth in the form of food. The food was transformed into energy by the digestive system, initially by the mother, and then by the individual after birth. The energy fuels the cells of the body to build and sustain physical life. Human life, however, is far more than a collection of energized cells that were formed out of clay. The physical body does not end at the outer layer of skin. It is connected to the multidimensional construct of encapsulating energy which can be viewed as the body of the Spirit.

In the physical world, science would explain that electrons, protons, and neutrons interact with the brain to create images within the consciousness. These images are the result of light being passed through the eyes, reflected on the retina, and transferred to the brain by the optic nerve. They mirror material objects which the brain then interprets as "physical reality."

Thought (the process of thinking) also results in the creation of images using protons, neutrons, and electrons to interact with the brain. Images which form in the brain, no matter the source, result from the same process: the interaction of electrons, protons, and neutrons. The difference between thought and physical reality lies in the source of light. The images created by thought result from light emerging from the Spirit mirroring non-physical objects, whereas "physical reality" results from reflected earthly light (such as the sun, moon, or a light bulb) which enters the brain through the eyes of flesh.

Whether the light emerges from the Spirit (Light Force) or reaches the brain through physical eyes, the resulting image inside the brain is the result of similar physics and chemistry. It is the mind that assesses the source of light using logic to determine whether the image mirrors the physical or non-physical.

Each experience, activity or thought in the physical world is mirrored by a corresponding non-physical image or framework. A number of such frameworks would be associated with every individual's life. The collection of frameworks exists within the layers of energy which encapsulates the physical body. This energy is not perceivable by human senses since it exists in a non-physical form.

Within the encapsulating construct, Spiritual Love circulates between the physical and non-physical. Truth, the subject of this section, is the material or building block of the non-physical structure of human life. These are the structures which are set aside in order to achieve the state of stillness which occurs during the practice of meditation.

Each person experiences life differently. This is based on belief systems, education, likes and dislikes, morals, financial status, etcetera. Each situation encountered in life emerges from parameters such as these. Relationships, for example, are based on such parameters. During the course of a relationship, if feelings change, then the dynamics of the situation would also change.

Two individuals may share common feelings such as hope, peace, love, acceptance, truth, patience, creativity, abundance, and joy. If attitudes towards any of these feelings change, then the dynamics of the relationship would also change. It could result in physical changes where the individuals no longer cohabit. It would also have an impact on the non-physical structure mirroring the relationship, which was created out of the dynamics between the two people. When a couple formulates a plan to live together, their aspirations result in thoughts and ideas that express their Truth. As these manifest in physical life, a mirror image is also reflected in the non-physical realm.

When an architect designs a house or a bridge, it would first appear in the non-physical realm before being transcribed onto paper. The formulation of thought into ideas and finally a completed design can be viewed as the expression of the architect's Truth.

If the non-physical structure created from the dynamics between two people was built with Truth, it holds the potential to grow from the adjustments due to changes or disturbances. Any structure, built by anyone, upon a foundation of Truth, will have the potential to survive and grow no matter what is encountered.

Truth can be viewed as the "bricks" which create non-physical existence. These bricks can be manipulated by the thoughts of individuals in the physical world, to shape and reshape existence.

The soul, which lives on beyond physical death, is created from a collection of non-physical structures mirroring physical life. The application of Truth and Love results in structures without karmic imprint. Soul structures enter the consciousness during the state of stillness, presenting the opportunity to re-create or reassemble the structures that hold a karmic imprint.

When asked, "What is Truth", perhaps the Nazarene master would have explained that Truth is the fabric of a reality which was created by choice. Perhaps He would have explained further that prayer (meditation) is a tool which can be used to disassemble and rebuild physical and non-physical life, using the materials of Love and Truth.

PART THIRTEEN

Fear

The word "fear" appears in the King James Version of the *Holy Bible* almost one thousand times. It would suggest that "fear" is addressed as a key element in a book which is believed by many to be designed as a guide for living. One notable example is when John wrote *"There is no fear in love; but perfect love casteth out fear: because fear hath torment. He that feareth is not made perfect in love." (1 John 4:18, Holy Bible, King James Version)*. Another example is from the writings of a young man who was later called King David. *"Yea, though I walk through the valley of the shadow of death, I will fear no evil: for thou art with me; thy rod and thy staff they comfort me." (Psalm 23:4, Holy Bible, King James Version)*. David also writes, *"Though an host should encamp against me, my heart shall not fear." (Psalm 27:3, Holy Bible, King James Version)*.

In the first passage, John explains fear and Spiritual Love do not coexist. For example, if "fear" is involved in the dynamics between two people, then the Love which is shared is not perfect. For example, someone may choose to hide events or lifestyles of the past due to fear of being judged. Perfect Love cannot exist where fear has crept in.

David looks at "fear" from a different perspective. He talks about facing life challenges without "fear". If "fear" emerges when life is under the direction of the Life Force, it would be dissolved by Love and Truth. Fear can emerge from the root, sacral or solar plexus chakras. Facing any challenge in life, like the fear of being judged for example, can be overcome by choosing to filter the energy through the heart chakra, the center of Love. Truth holds the power to manifest choice. Perfect Love holds the power to dissolve fear.

The greatest power a human being commands is the freedom to choose. Due to the nature of duality, each situation encountered in life offers multiple choices. Each choice would lead in a different direction and create different situations. The choice may be based on logic offered by the mind, or on Love and Truth offered by the Life Force. Although the mind hears the gentle call of the Life Force to "follow me," the mind feels comfortable with logic and repeating familiar patterns. Often, these are based on "fear".

The safe or convenient pathways keep life in a holding pattern. The way of the Life Force, however, should be the obvious choice since it leads to personal development, success, and happiness. Fear of change stands in the way. Fear holds the power to influence choice by creating a wall that stands between the holding pattern and the true nature of the self.

Fear itself is dual in nature. The examples from the *Holy Bible* present the negative and destructive side. Whenever this form of "fear" is involved in the dynamics of a situation, old karmic patterns are present or new ones are being created within the soul. Fear also has a positive and creative side. It will present itself as a survival tool. In moments of danger, the body reacts by pumping adrenaline into the bloodstream. The heart rate increases, respiration rate increases, and pupils dilate. It is an instinctive reaction. The body is prepared for a "fight or flight" response.

In ancient times, "fight or flight" was the instinctive reaction to an unexpected encounter with any form of danger, such as a hungry predator. In current times, observing the domain of life on the earth, "fight or flight" is still the instinctive reaction to danger. Humans, however, have adapted to meet new forms of danger, such as changes to climate and food source. Within the scientific community, evolution typically refers to changes in the biology of a species. Humans have also adapted to meet the challenges of a changing mental landscape. Although "fight or flight" remains the instinctive reaction, tools, such as guns, knives, vehicles, etc., were created to address physical dangers. Humans learnt how to use their minds to develop more effective forms of defence.

In present day society, changes occur quickly enough that over the course of a single lifetime, one can observe shifts in areas such as belief systems, morality, and the physical condition. Even greater change can be observed when comparing the present day to the generations of parents and grandparents. The quality of food, air, and water have changed, largely due to pollution from industry, transportation, and factory farming. Cancers, cardiovascular disease, obesity, and diabetes have become commonplace in western society. Many of these conditions were uncommon before the industrial age. In addition to the impact industrialisation brought to the physical condition, changes can also be observed in morality, belief systems, attitudes, expectations, etc. If such significant changes can be observed over a short period of time, one can only imagine the enormous changes that have occurred in the framework of life over many thousands of years of human history.

How has the "fear", which resulted in a "fight or flight" reaction, change over time? Considering that humans have mentally developed and grown over many thousands of years, it's no surprise enormous changes in the mental landscape have occurred. Fear became more than an instinctive response when danger was present. It became a tool to protect the fragile, evolving mental framework of the person as well.

The Life Force shining through the lens of the evolving mind brought changes to the physical as well as the mental, emotional, and spiritual environments. Consequently, the root chakra, the area of survivability, adapted to this changing environment. Survivability, its key function, which originally protected physicality, took on the additional responsibility of protecting the evolving psychological framework reflected within the consciousness.

For example, many face the challenges of an economic jungle (finding a job or other means of earning money) which must be navigated in order to survive in today's society. Basic necessities such as food, housing, and clothing depend on access to sufficient money. The need for money or the lack of necessities that it can buy activated emotions which precipitated the "fear" of insufficiency. No one wants to experience food shortages, absence of adequate clothing, or lack of a safe and comfortable home. This fear created the desire for abundance and hoarding. The result was a desire to acquire excess, which is the definition for "greed". While "instinctive fear" protects physicality, what can be described as "psychological fear" evolved out of greed.

"Greed" is a word that feels harsh, and no one wants to feel that it is part of their personality. The need for excess, however, is an intrinsic part of today's society. "Fear" is also a word that feels harsh when it applies to the nature of personal life.

Learning about fear, its connection to greed, and how it relates to personal life will shed light on the intrinsic nature of our personality and perhaps offer an avenue of change, which could impact evolution and devolution of the soul. Fear, however, goes beyond navigating the economic jungle. The fear, which can be experienced in today's society, presents itself with many different names, shows its face in the most unexpected time and place, or influences situations without being seen. When it manifests, its tentacles are prevalent—power, domination, control, slavery, and violence are just a few. Schools of thought, such as economics, political science, international investment, business administration, and even policing, are based upon fear and are blindly accepted as a way of life. It has become integral in the mode of operating within society, so much that it feels normal when it occurs.

How each individual prepares for the challenges presented by fear will be unique. It is a personal war, representing the greatest challenge one will ever face—the self or psyche. It is difficult because the psyche knows how to hide its own weaknesses. The war will consist of many battles, one for each element of the soul that was created by karma. These are elements which do not resonate with the Love and Truth of the Spirit, but instead emerged out of challenges from the past where the path of fear was chosen instead of Love and Truth. In the earlier example where the past was hidden out of fear of judgement, a karmic element within the soul would result and remain to be faced in the future.

The body prepares for whatever is held within the mind. In other words, when an intention to change aspects of the psyche is held within the mind, the Life Force prepares the physical body by activating the chakras. During the practice of meditation, the Life Force can be directed to shine through a lens of objectivity, illuminating different chakras, causing Love and Truth to become the motivating force instead of fear. By reflecting on the day ahead, the mind and the consciousness can also prepare for potential challenges.

Due to the nature of his writing, the psalmist David, would have faced a life of great challenges. Practicing meditation prepared him for difficult encounters. When he wrote, *"Yea, though I walk through the valley of the shadow of death, I will fear no evil: for thou art with me; thy rod and thy staff they comfort me." (Psalm 23:4, Holy Bible, King James Version),* David sees evil in the valley of shadows as situations which hold the potential to create karma. He is reassured by the knowledge that Truth and Love flowing from the Life Force can conquer fear and yield victory over every situation.

Part Fourteen
Death

"O death, where is thy sting? O grave, where is thy victory? The sting of death is sin; and the strength of sin is the law." (1 Corinthians 15:55-56, Holy Bible, King James Version).

It is easy to lose sight of who we are as human beings. We are all part of the ecosystem of the planet. All forms of life share the planet equally as brothers and sisters from one mother: the earth. All breathe the same air, drink the same water, and are clothed and fed from one source.

The earth's bounty is abundant and provides sufficiently for everyone. Humans hold a perspective of superiority over all other life forms, and for some, this notion of superiority applies to other humans as well. Humans have pillaged and polluted the earth, which is not only our home, but also our very source of life. It provides our food, water, air, clothing, and housing.

The world is always changing and evolving. Humankind, however, appears to be devolving based on the collective disrespect of the planet and other life forms, including—and especially—the self. All life on the planet falls under the same physical principles. All are born, all live, and then all eventually die. All beings have bodies created out of the dust of the planet. Humans, however, tend to view their own species as different—the power of the mind being the distinguishing feature. The brain in conjunction with the mind is like a massive computer which can be used in the most amazing ways, such as conceiving, designing, and building something as complicated as an automobile. It ignores the truth: that each life form has a free and equal share of the numerous resources the planet offers. Beyond using resources for what one needs, the human mind desires and chooses to horde, steal, dominate, and instigate wars for selfish purposes. In this regard, the world has become a dangerous place at times because of the potential of negativity's power to destroy. Not everyone, however, is devolving. Many have awakened to this reality and have chosen a path of change by honouring personal convictions and becoming living examples of the true nature of life, which is Love and Truth.

Within the complex ecosystem of the universe, the sun rises each day to awaken life. At the moment when the light emerges over the horizon, a dance begins. Birds seek out the highest branches of the tallest tree hoping to be the first to experience the moment when the stillness and silence of the night is transformed into a bright and bustling landscape. The energizing rays of the sun begin a journey across the sky, nourishing the earth.

Passion within is awakened by the beauty exuded from the natural rhythm of nature as night cycles into day and the earth revolves around the sun. The experience of such passion is a manifestation of the Spirit or Life Force shining within the physical body. The life experienced here on Earth is only part of an even more complex ecosystem where Spirit journeys through the realms. Each earthly experience is a minute slice of time out of an eternal journey. It is a journey where the passion of the Spirit is experienced like a revolving door between realms. Spirit formed a vessel out of clay, the dust of the earth, in order to have a sojourn here and experience the manifestation of its passion. In other words, through physical birth, Spirit created the opportunity to experience its expression here on Earth.

The concept of eternity is an illusion created by the mind to define infinite time. The length of a life can be defined in years, months, weeks, days, hours, minutes, and seconds. Moments of time are less important than the sequence of experiences undertaken and achievements made during that lifetime. If time is removed from the equation, only the achievements remain. Thus, the Spirit views a whole lifetime as a single moment filled with achievements.

Death is generally not part of the framework of everyday thought. Within the recesses of the mind, there is an acknowledgement that physical death will play a role sometime in the future. The clothing of clay, the crucible of the Spirit, and instrument of the mind will one day be shed. This Truth is ignored by the healthy and happy with a "live from moment-to-moment" philosophy. It is a practice where personal mortality (death) is not included when life-navigating choices are being made. Life is based on the concept that there is always more time. This concept emerges from the Truth held within the subconscious, that the Life Force is eternal and continues to exist beyond the revolving door of birth and death.

In his letter to the church in Corinth, the apostle Paul shared in 1 Corinthians 15:55-56, that the "sting" of death or physical death is not to be feared. It is not the end of existence but simply part of the ecosystem of eternal life. The concept of "sin" can be equated with the laws of karma where choices lead to devolution and create fear. Victory over the fear of death emerges from manifesting Love and Truth.

PART FIFTEEN
Re-birth

The complexity of the human body is illustrated in books such as Henry Gray's *Gray's Anatomy*, first published in 1858. The anatomist describes the various components of the body and their function. The basic building blocks are cells, of which trillions are required. At a microscopic level, each cell is composed of trillions of atoms which work as a unit.

Organs are built from cells. The body is kept alive by organs all working in unison. For example, the brain is the command centre, the lungs take oxygen into the body, the heart pumps oxygenated blood through the body, the stomach receives food that nourishes the body, and so on. However, the functioning of the human body is far more complex than the synchronous operation of a few organs. There is far more to the story.

Glands are also built from cells. The endocrine system is a network of glands which manufacture hormones. Hormones are circulated through the bloodstream to carry out specific functions. Feelings, which originate from the mind's intentions and are experienced in daily activities, activate the endocrine system to produce hormones. For example, situations that invoke fear will activate the adrenal gland (among others) to create a "fight, flight, or panic reaction". The thyroid gland releases hormones that help maintain balance in the areas of the bowels and heart. An imbalance can result in hypertension, constipation, or diarrhea, among other ailments. The sensations created within the body, when communicating through voice or otherwise, are among the factors that impact the functioning of the thyroid. When the desire to manifest Truth underlines communication, hormones necessary for creating balance within the body are released into the bloodstream. In comparison, a personality entangled in deception will release hormones which result in an imbalance. Notwithstanding accidents and environmental conditions, there is a direct relationship between the longevity of a human body and the mind's connection with Truth. In other words, the people who live the longest have a mental framework underlined by Truth. Total balance is created within the human body when the mind's intention is underlined by Love and Truth.

The human body is truly a marvel. Each cell is like a whole universe. The microscopic vastness, complexity, and detail is much like looking at the sky on a starry night, wondering how far it extends and what mysteries it holds. Scientific minds define the size of the cosmos by what can be measured or observed. The knowledge base continues to grow with new discoveries. Logic dictates that the cosmos extends beyond the confines of the mind's perception. The Life Force that animates the physical body, also exists in a place outside the realm which the mind is capable of perceiving.

In order to embrace the opportunity to experience the physical realm, Spirit joins with a human body at the time of physical birth. Just as death is not the end, birth is not the beginning—rather, it is part of the continuous flow where the physical and ethereal states are experienced together. A single lifetime is a series of experiences orchestrated by the mind, experienced by the body, and directed by the Spirit. From the perspective of the Spirit, a physical lifetime is but a moment filled with experiences and opportunities. Within that moment, free will grants the potential to make choices that will lead to either evolution or devolution. On a larger scale, the current state of humanity is the result of this free will.

Karma is often viewed as a force generated by a person's actions, consequences of which determine the nature of the person's next existence. The Truth about karma is often misunderstood as a force that is beyond control. It is the Spirit, however, which enacts karma and chooses how life will unfold in the revolving doorway of physical birth and death.

The physical world can be viewed as a grand theatre in which all of humanity are actors. Parents, friends, teachers, siblings, fiancés, and even strangers all play a role in the drama of life. Each individual is the director of a personal narrative. The performances of today will determine how life unfolds tomorrow and whether success and happiness are written into the script. The mind is only capable of seeing a single perspective of the drama where the cast and relationships are circumstantial, but this is far from the whole story. The rest of the story unfolds with events that take place in the realms between physical death and birth.

The soul is a crucible for experiences orchestrated by the mind, the effects of those experiences, and the associated emotions. The soul survives physical death and is eternally connected to the Spirit. Multiple souls are associated with each Spirit, one for each lifetime. Each soul can be identified by a name, the one associated with the physical body during the time on the earth. For example, the collective experiences of someone called Mary or Jack live on as unique souls associated with their respective Spirits. All that is gained or lost remains within the crucible until the opportunity to make changes is presented.

The Spirit reviews past lives and selects the events to be experienced in the next physical incarnation—choosing to repeat those which resulted in devolution. Reliving the events offers the opportunity to choose the next actions differently, giving a devolving soul an opportunity to change, grow, and realign with the Spirit. Evolution of the soul is returning to the state of oneness with the Spirit.

Prior to birth, a drama would be organized which would offer this opportunity. A cast would be selected with members who are willing to help. Most of the members would have shared prior life experiences and be connected by a bond of Love. The cast would likewise have the opportunity to grow and change. The drama would orchestrate events that would create a physical and emotional environment mirroring a previous experience. The place on Earth would be selected with a suitable political, economic, social, and moral environment. A timeline for the series of births into the physical world would be established and grandparents, parents, siblings, and friends would queue to enter the stage.

The life currently being lived by each person on Earth is the unfolding of this drama. It begins at birth with a clean slate where the mind is disconnected from memories of past events. Each life is navigated by the free will to choose. As the drama unfolds, choice will determine whether there will be success or failure. When personal choice is based on direction given by the gentle voice heard within the silence of the consciousness, the drama will unfold as designed prior to birth. The person would successfully evolve through change and growth. The inverse is also true. Ignoring inner guidance and leading a life based on fear will result in devolution. The laws of karma evolved out of the eternal Love, which created opportunities to reverse devolution through such dramas.

Imagine a story about a rich man and a beggar. It is easy to judge someone who is wearing tattered clothing, is unkempt, drunk, or unpleasantly fragrant, especially if they are occupying the doorstep of your home. A drama is unfolding with a beggar and rich man who were once brothers. Both agreed to help each other in the next physical incarnation. The rich man needs to learn about compassion. The beggar needs to experience poverty. As the drama unfolds, one was born to a family of great wealth, the other was born to less fortunate circumstances and became a beggar in the street.

As the story progresses, every day the beggar asks the rich man for food and is ignored. The appeals for food become stronger and more emotional as the days go by. One day, the beggar was not there. The rich man learns he has died. All the wealth in the world cannot negate the feeling of anguish and remorse. That very night, he dreams about a wise man who could heal people by feeding them. He immediately understands the meaning of the dream. He is the wise man and the less fortunate are symbolized by the sick. Healing the sick means finding a way to help the poor. He converts his house to a home for the homeless. Guided by a dream, the rich man learns how to Love unconditionally by expressing the compassion he feels in his heart.

The law of karma as expressed in this drama, gives the rich man the opportunity to express Love in the form of compassion. It also gives the poor man the opportunity to experience long-lasting suffering and the need for patience. It is an opportunity for the soul to evolve by aligning its values with the Spirit or Life Force.

In another example, a child with a congenital disease enters the physical world presenting unexpected challenges to new parents. In this drama, the child chose this life to provide an opportunity for the parents to learn how to Love unconditionally by being patient, kind, caring, and humble.

The unfolding drama of life is not always personal. It can extend to include families, organizations, churches, and even countries. For example, those affected by natural disasters or even wars are being offered the opportunity to dissolve karma created by similar situations in the past.

It is easy to judge the drama of life when the mind is not aware of the whole story. Through the revolving doorway of life, birth offers the repeating opportunity to embrace the true nature of the Spirit in all situations with the free will to choose Love and Truth. Such is the vast power of the Life Force as it extends beyond the far reaches of the Universe to experience physical existence here on earth.

Birth

Sparkling, the world becomes.
The world is.
Dancing with the rainbow,
Dawn is everywhere.
Birds sing to the new day.
Smiling faces wave greetings.
The melody of a song, I am.
A spark of light, I am.
Nothing, everything sparkles.
I close my eyes and breathe to embrace it all.
Oh!
Clouds!
Is this dawn?

ABOUT MEDITATION

The dancing stops.
It is a new world.
My eyes slowly open.

Why am I here?
Where did the flowers go?
Where did the rainbow go?
Who am I?
What is this place?

But here I am.
This is me.
This is all of me.
My new world.

I cry because I remember,
But soon forget.
And I hug my Mamma.

Part Sixteen
Being

Beyond birth, one exists. Choices made during the state of existence determine the nature of life. Human nature at any given moment is determined by choices based on patterns that have been previously established within the psyche, or based on the free will to choose differently. The psyche is developed during the formative years, at a time when the receptive mind is imprinted with patterns from its surroundings. Parents, friends, teachers, siblings, church, and school all play roles in the formation of the adolescent's nature. Karmic patterns established in past lives also play a role in the nature of the psyche. Patterns from past lives are stored in the subconscious and become accessible when they are needed. Both the conscious and subconscious influence personal choice and thereby, the nature of life. Furthermore, while daily activities may follow societal programming, the response to new and unexpected situations is influenced by the subconscious. In these new situations, when patterns from familiar experiences cannot provide answers, there is an immediate and involuntary response from the subconscious. The mind takes a back seat, allowing introspection in the moment, which allows access to the vast storehouse of the subconscious. The resulting choice is often based on themes established during the past. For example, Love and Truth would influence a current decision if they were also chosen in the past. Past lives that were based on fear will also influence current situations with facets such as greed, subjugation, or desire for control. The response from introspection will feel instinctive or natural. It would take place without one realizing it happened in the moment.

The nature of the psyche does not negate the power of free will. The direction a person follows is determined by the individual's choice; therefore, a person has the freedom to choose the next steps, regardless of the nature of the psyche. Performing daily activities will generally follow patterns in the conscious mind; this is the result of personal choice.

The freedom to choose is available to everyone at each moment. Furthermore, choosing a path of inaction or having a passive response is also a conscious choice. A person's situation in the present is the result of past choices. The human condition is a result of personal responsibility. The freedom to change is a choice which is incumbent upon each individual.

Exercising the freedom to choose is the greatest power an individual can wield. It transcends the mind and the subconscious. It transcends all that is true or false in the personification of human life. Change is possible by simply choosing a different direction and making the choice to remain dedicated to this path. Choosing to personify Love and Truth means embracing the true nature of the self. It is simply being normal. It is a pathway which will create a state of happiness. Love and Truth are facets of the indwelling Spirit and happiness is the natural state of the Spirit.

This feeling of happiness is a compass that points towards the indwelling Spirit. The purpose for being in the physical realm can be fulfilled by using this compass to navigate life.

Part Seventeen

Forgiveness

In 1947, clay jars filled with scrolls were found in caves beside the Dead Sea. One of the scrolls was entitled, *The Prayer to Our Father*. It was written in the ancient Aramaic language, but today there are many translations. In western society, one of the most common versions is known as *The Lord's Prayer*. Translations appear in the *Book of Matthew* and the *Book of Luke* in the *Holy Bible*. Matthew writes, *"And forgive us our debts, as we forgive our debtors." (Matthew 6:12, Holy Bible, King James Version)*. The words used by Luke are similar. *"And forgive us our debts; for we also forgive every one that is indebted to us." (Luke 11:4, Holy Bible, King James Version)*.

In today's society, the idea of forgiveness is part of the psyche of most. In the west, the phrases "I am sorry, please forgive me" and "I forgive you" are standard responses in certain situations. Uttering such words is often considered the resolution. It may be sufficient in that moment, but dynamics of true forgiveness are vastly different.

When someone offends, the desire to restore the relationship leads to seeking forgiveness. The desire to seek forgiveness is based on the state of the offender's conscience. Saying, "I am sorry, please forgive me" or "I forgive you" does not necessarily mean the offender is truly repentant. The truly penitent will first make amends before uttering those words. For example, if someone betrays trust by stealing money, it should be repaid in full with interest before attempting to seek forgiveness. Furthermore, the offender should make life changes to ensure the offence will not be repeated. In circumstances which involve bodily injury, infidelity, or death, where avenues for recompense are rarely possible, the process of forgiveness will transcend this physical life. The state of the conscience and personal responsibility will determine whether the laws of karma will be enacted. Thinking back, the beggar who gave his life by suffering through hunger repaid a karmic debt. In a past life, he had allowed others to die from hunger. Since forgiveness was not an option, his conscience dictated that he needed to experience the same in order to understand the true meaning of selfless Love.

Consider another example where there were two sons in a family. They exemplified brotherly love by walking the streets arm in arm when they were children. Unknown to the younger brother, the older had the makings of a crook. The younger brother realized this upon the death of their father, when an inheritance was left to be shared amongst the family. Although the younger brother had no desire for money, honour dictated that their father's wishes should be followed. However, this was not possible because the older brother had already orchestrated a path to steal all the money and estranged himself from the rest of the family. The younger brother tried to persuade his older brother to honour their father's wishes, but failed. A court battle was not an option to be considered. Instead, the outcome was accepted. Rekindling a brotherly relationship failed after several attempts by the younger. It was clear the older brother was satisfied with the feeling he outwitted the rest of the family. He did not seek forgiveness nor did he return the stolen money.

The younger brother tried to look through the eyes of the older in order to understand his reason for cheating. It took time, patience, and reflection, but it eventually became clear. The older brother's education, immediate family values, and life experiences with friends and colleagues had created a mental framework overshadowed by the fear of insufficiency, which led to greed. Patterns created by karma would also impact his choices.

In the bitter moments of a personal challenge, it is difficult to understand the choices others make. The younger brother was giving the older brother an opportunity to choose differently, but the older brother fell into old habits. Furthermore, his capacity to feel remorse was not rekindled. Forgiveness and recompense were not options he was considering.

Acceptance without any conditions is an expression associated with the purest form of Love. Accepting the injustice of the older brother or acting out of compassion to help the unfortunate (the beggar sitting at the rich man's door) is an act of Love. Here on Earth, the human experience is an amazing opportunity to challenge the self to Love unconditionally. Personal interaction acts like a mirror reflecting the true nature of a person. The experience with the older brother is an opportunity to witness the unfolding of his psyche. It is an opportunity to challenge himself to transcend old patterns. In this case, he failed. It is also an opportunity for the younger brother to manifest unconditional acceptance and dissolve karma.

In a perfect world, the term "forgiveness" would be replaced by "acceptance". When the wronged expresses acceptance without any condition or expectation, it is an act of the perfect Love as described by the apostle John *(1 John 4:18, Holy Bible, King James Version)*. It gives the offender, the one seeing forgiveness, the opportunity to experience remorse and make amends. The wronged does not have power over "forgiveness"—only the ability to express acceptance, which creates a framework where the offender can choose to change.

The Lord's Prayer was given by the Nazarene master when his disciples asked Him to teach them to pray. According to the *Gospel of Luke*, the fifth line addresses the subject of "forgiveness". *"And forgive us our debts; for we also forgive every one that is indebted to us."* (Luke 11:4, *Holy Bible, King James Version)*. The master used the words "debt" and "indebted" as symbols for situations which result in the need for recompense.

The older brother is indebted to the rest of his siblings, not simply because of the money he stole, but for an action which created disharmony. The rich man had the means to relieve the suffering of the beggar but did not act and therefore became indebted. The individual who hid information about the past created a debt by creating disharmony in the relationship.

The chakra system of the human body plays a role in the act of forgiveness. Fear, which manifests greed, in the case of the older brother, emerged from an imbalance in the first chakra, the area of survivability. The Love which manifests acceptance emerges from the fourth chakra. The inner power or will to act emerges from the third chakra. Manifesting the truth which emerges from within is associated with the fifth chakra. Focusing on Love and Truth during the practice of meditation can bring the chakras into balance. The imbalance within the third chakra, which resulted in greed, can be transformed by the fourth chakra into Love and Truth.

Part Eighteen
The Book of Errors

Society is a group of vastly different individuals interacting with each other because of common interests or to achieve a common purpose. The same definition applies to nations, families, organizations, and even personal relationships where people share common activities, traditions or goals.

Distinct from the whole is the role of the individual; each person has a different function and coexists with the collective, propelled by personal responsibility for current and future states of being. New choices that emerge from the practice of meditation, however, will result in a path which does not conform to traditional social behaviours. When such a path is followed, the entire collective feels the effect, just as the entire body feels the impact when a single cell ails. On the journey that emerges from practice of meditation, life will not synchronize with the collective, as the individual will forge unique personal perspectives and face the challenge of being different.

What did Paul the Apostle mean when he used the words, *"For all have sinned and fall short of the glory of God"? (Romans 3:23, Holy Bible, King James Version)*. It means that within society, no one is perfect. All have erred. Somewhere in the past, the direction of life changed due to personal choices made in error. The Spirit is always willing but the flesh can be weak *(Matthew 26:41, Holy Bible, King James Version)*, resulting in errors. Errors are the consequences of choices based on fear instead of Love or Truth. These errors are responsible for the current state of being and can be identified while meditating. Correcting errors will become the objective of life's journey.

All that is understood about life and its purpose is limited by the capabilities set forth by the mind. Much like a computer, the capabilities of each person are defined by a series of programs created by the mind and held within the brain. For example, morality is one of these "programs" which has been coded with influence from parents and society. Life is dynamic in nature since programs can be added, changed, or deleted. These changes are a function of free will.

Exercising the free will to choose is the innate power that enacts self-determination. In the current state of being, life is determined by the "programs" within the mind. The practice of meditation can be used to bypass these programs and access reality beyond the confines of the mind, the source of Truth. Totality, experiencing Truth fully, exists beyond the confines of the mind.

Just as a computer can be upgraded, so too can the mind be developed. Installing new software on top of an old operating system can cause errors. Technical experts always advise to first erase the old operating system and its programs before installing new software. This method results in more efficient and reliable operating systems. To fulfill the purpose for being here on Earth, patterns, or programs defined by the mind must first be disassembled, removed, and then intentionally rebuilt from the ground up. As described earlier, this process symbolizes death and rebirth. When the Apostle Paul speaks of the "glory of God", it is a symbol for the oneness between physical life and the indwelling Life Force achieved by the correction of errors. Restoring this "glory" is a symbol for "rebirth".

On life's journey of reprogramming, the indwelling Spirit will assume the driver's seat. Physical and mental adjustments, in conjunction with the practice of meditation, will result in a shift in consciousness where the mechanics of the psyche will become visible, revealing errors that were engineered into its structure. Parameters will also become visible to reverse engineer the structure so it can be rebuilt with new programming using a source code of Love and Truth, thereby dissolving the errors held within the mechanics of the mind. It will become clear that the errors being encountered were the architects of an old way of life and must be reassessed within a new paradigm. The innate desire to manifest Love and Truth will be compelling.

Hasten not to act impulsively but instead take a deep breath and exercise patience, yielding command to the Spirit. Observe the feelings that are emerging from within. Observe the attitudes, emotions, and expectations that are emerging from the mind. Observe the physical reaction within the body. This is the juncture between reliving old patterns and rebuilding the mechanics of the psyche upon a new foundation. It is an opportunity to regain what was lost in a past that was seeded by fear.

A journal is an invaluable tool during the process of transformation. Keep detailed notes of errors as they are revealed through the state of objectivity created by the practice of meditation. Use the notes to analyze the errors and make plans to correct them. For example, the one that hid the truth can write all the details of the error in a journal for later analysis. A method of correcting the error can be determined through introspection or while meditating. Once the error is corrected, the process can also be added to the journal.

Include the date, time, location, and outline the roles of all involved. Describe your attitude, the state of your conscience, and any feelings experienced before, during, and after the error is corrected. This information is a valuable tool for reflection. Solutions may emerge at the moment. Some answers may be obvious, whereas others may appear while meditating or in a dream state. Be patient and persevere. Answers will come. On this journey, looking through the eyes of the indwelling Spirit will forever be a source of Truth. Include solutions as they appear and also when successfully applied. The journal will create a road map of progress and ultimately become a personal manual of instruction.

Healing is a silent and invisible force that occurs during the process of re-engineering the psyche. Certain errors will manifest as physical or mental conditions. Dissolving the error will consequently clear the condition and enable the body to restore itself to a natural state. Healing may be invisible to the mind and seen as a miracle. (Occurrences that the mind cannot rationalize within its existing framework of logic are viewed as miracles or magic.) Certain conditions connected to karmic issues may be healed in the current lifetime, while others may require multiple lives to be addressed. There are conditions that may be the result of personal choice due to a karmic commitment. Many of these remain unexplained in the medical field, such as cancer, Alzheimer's, Parkinson's, schizophrenia, genetic diseases, and autoimmune disorders, to list just a few.

When facing current life situations with new attitudes, situations will always appear to challenge both the mind and the body. Avoid negative thoughts and instead view them as opportunities to dissolve errors. Victory will be dependent on the ability to manifest the power of free will to maintain course. Know strength and courage lie deep within, and victory is only a choice. Nurture an attitude of expectancy where the road being travelled is paved with discarded errors.

Know the elements of life that lie within and learn how to recognize them. Love, Truth, peace, patience, and creativity are all facets of the indwelling Spirit. Like seeds, they wait patiently to be nurtured so they can grow and blossom into happiness. Learn how to recognize when life is on a pathway navigated by the compass pointing to happiness. Embrace the opportunities at hand by being aware and vigilant at all times.

During the process of correcting errors, choose a new name, one which represents the reprogrammed person. Visualize a rock that is sturdy and unmovable; this is the rock of Truth which symbolizes the new person being created. Meditate upon the desire to find a name and allow it to emerge from within. The mind will seek to intervene and offer many names. Be thankful for the kindness offered and respectfully decline. With an attitude of expectancy, the answer will come. A name will appear in the consciousness, one which resonates with the commitment to the journey. Grace, Patience, Rock, Hope, Kind One, Penitent, Joy, Faith, or Gentle One are examples of a few names that may emerge. Once selected, honour this name. Share it with no one, for it is a symbol of a sacred being. Hold the name within the consciousness at the start of each meditation.

Nurture the virtues of the Spirit. The mind and body must always be prepared, for the time and place of the next challenge is unknown. Do not be caught unprepared. External aids can serve as reminders to always be alert. For example, an arm band made of beads or seeds was used by the Choctaw Nation of Oklahoma to symbolize the start of a new journey or a new commitment. Another external aid could be a mantra such as "I am Love" or "I am Truth." Mantras can be effective when repeated at scheduled times, such as before sleep, in the morning, or before each meal. It will serve as a reminder to stay on course.

Again, it is a personal journey and all aspects should remain private, including the mantra or any other symbol. Otherwise, there is a potential to become prideful, thereby allowing the valuable energy held within the purpose to escape. Staying on course will always be a challenge. Personal aids will be unique to each person. Questions will arise from friends and family regarding the new source of happiness and the new path. Be forthcoming if the questions are earnest. Be not prideful in knowing that at this stage of the journey, the student becomes the teacher.

The Light of the Heart

The anticipation of light fills the heart
Upon awakening in the early hours of dawn.

Crimson and gold and soon a burst of white
to embrace all of creation.

It is our reality
And it happens every day.

Every single day,
There is the opportunity to awaken to the light,
The joyous all-embracing light
That shines, not only from the east,
But from the deepest corners of the hearts,
For the heart is made of light.

And as you walk upon this earth,
You are the dawn
In the life of those you touch.
Amen.

Part Nineteen
Healing

Perfect health is the natural state of being for any life form. The natural equilibrium that maintains health can be disturbed by factors such as accidents or the environment. Personal choices can also affect the mind, which will disturb the physical equilibrium and result in disease.

The psalmist was addressing the diseases when he wrote the words, *"Bless the Lord, O my soul, and forget not all his benefits, who forgives all your iniquity, who heals all your diseases, who redeems your life from the pit, who crowns you with steadfast love and mercy, who satisfies you with good so that your youth is renewed like the eagle's." (Psalm 103:1-5, Holy Bible, King James Version)*. Healing of mental and physical conditions starts with forgiveness. The psalmist is cognizant that healing occurs when errors are corrected by applying the Love and Truth which emerge from the Life Force.

The process of healing is activated by focusing on the Love that energizes life and fuels the desire to correct errors. It is the Love that flows from the Life Force and is present during the state of silence when meditating *("Bless the Lord, O my soul, and forget not all his benefits")*. This Love can be held within the consciousness and carried into daily activities where it can be used to activate healing by correcting errors *("who forgives all your iniquity, who heals all your diseases, who redeems your life from the pit")*. The desire to make choices that will result in change and growth will fill the consciousness *("who crowns you with steadfast love and mercy")*.

Love does not control, nor does it have expectations. Love accepts all without condition. Within the collective or in personal relationships, a bond of Love, based on mutual acceptance, yields harmony and growth. It is this form of Love that recognizes the capacity to make errors and offers the opportunity to heal them in one another. Love deeply and completely, for the energy of Love that emerges from the heart will illuminate every cell within and expand outward to touch the hearts and lives of others. The desire to dissolve karma or correct errors in order to manifest the fullness of life *("who satisfies you with good so that your youth is renewed like the eagle's.")* is an expression of the Love that flows from the Life Force.

When psalm 103 was written, the psalmist was cognizant of mental and physical afflictions and mindful of the process of healing them. Perhaps his words were personal, or were offered advice due to an empathetic experience. The Truth offered applies in both situations.

Healing oneself starts with a desire to change. The objective view of life, which occurs during the meditative state of silence, which brings karmic patterns or errors into focus, will initiate the desire to replace them with Love and Truth. This desire can be manifested with a commitment to self and a dedicated practice of meditation.

To achieve the benefits of healing through meditation, a strict regimen is required where the practice occurs in the middle of the sleep cycle. For example, for someone that sleeps eight hours each night starting at 11:00PM, the best time to meditate would be 3:00AM. This allows for approximately four hours of sleep before and four hours after the practice. Sufficient sleep is necessary to maintain the equilibrium between the body, mind, and Life Force that is required for healing to take place. Therefore, choose a time that matches personal sleep patterns. The greatest benefits would be realized by practicing at the same time each day.

The body and the mind will adjust to the cycles of nature. Sleeping at night-time is natural as darkness is more conducive to sleep. The body and mind will also adjust to the rhythms created from daily routine.

Consider, for example, that the muscles, heart, and respiration will adjust by growing stronger to meet the needs of an athlete who runs every day. If it is done at a specific time, the body will be prepared for that moment with the needed energy. Likewise, a commitment to meditating at the same time each day will have its benefits. The body and mind will be prepared to remain in a state of silence for the selected period of time. A dedicated practice of meditation will improve the quality of the experience with greater clarity in recognizing karmic patterns or errors during the state of silence.

The relationship between the flow of energy within the body and meditation is cyclical. Meditation can help control the flow of energy; likewise, improving the flow of energy will improve the quality of meditations. The main pipeline that connects the brain with the rest of the body runs along the spinal column. Misalignment of a single vertebrae will result in blockages which impede the flow of energy. This can be caused by accidents, abuse, repetitive stress, or even poor posture. Removal of impediments can be achieved under the guidance of the indwelling Spirit, or alternatively, through chiropractic or osteopathic adjustments. There are practitioners who are familiar with such energy work.

Self-adjustment is possible while meditating, but it requires patience and faith in oneself. The adjustment can be achieved by yielding control of the physical body to the indwelling Spirit. To do this, ask the mind to take a back seat and remain silent.

The mind is always aware of conditions that result in a disturbance of the physical equilibrium, such as spinal misalignment. As a function of this body-consciousness, there will be an innate awareness of the procedures which will correct the disturbances. The awareness emerges while meditating as a feeling or desire to initiate certain movements. It may involve using the hands to apply pressure of a specific magnitude and direction. For example, the movements of the body may be reminiscent of a yoga posture.

When healing is held within the mind during meditation with an attitude of expectancy, the desire or feeling to initiate corrective movements will be spontaneous. The steps will percolate into the consciousness as an innate desire to manipulate the arms, legs, neck, head, or spine. Again, self-manipulation is performed by yielding control of the body to the Spirit. These adjustments cannot be forced or controlled. The mind will try to interfere every step of the way by injecting its own methods using logic for justification. Exercise restraint, for incorrect movements can result in harm. Success can be achieved by having faith in oneself and the indwelling Spirit.

Adjusting the body to improve energy flow is an ongoing process that occurs in conjunction with personal growth. Dedicate part of a meditation session to the purpose of physical self-adjustment once per week, at most. To initiate healing, assume a posture that will be conducive to physical adjustments. One such position is to sit on a firm but comfortable chair with the spine gently erect, the palms on the lap facing downwards, and the feet placed flat on the floor. Ask the mind to step aside and remain silent. Know that the mind is like a child with a short attention span and will quickly interfere. When this happens, be patient and gently ask the mind to return to its place of silence. Honour the mind by making mental notes to address the thoughts at a more conducive time.

Even if it is not an objective, the healing process will be activated with dedication to the practice of meditation. Success often occurs within the first few sessions. The feeling of elation after experiencing success will create a desire to repeat the process. Be patient, for the body will need time to complete the adjustment in order to fully heal itself. Dedicating only one session per week to healing will provide the body with enough time to heal.

One of the roles of the spine is the protection of the spinal cord. The spine is also the foundation of posture and enables the body to move or bend. The spinal cord connects the brain to the lower back and carries signals to and from the entire body. The signals are responsible for the movement and control of the entire body. The nervous system is connected to the endocrine, which in turn maps to energy centers of the chakra system. Each spinal adjustment will improve the flow of energy between the endocrine system and the Life Force. These centres will need time for the healing process to be completed. Healing can take up to seven days. Be sensitive to all physical conditions in order to become aware when the adjustments are complete.

As one becomes more proficient, the specified amount of time chosen to practice meditation will feel inadequate. As this happens, gradually increase the dedicated time by 5, 10, or 15 minutes. A total of sixty minutes is a sufficient goal. If there is a desire to go beyond one hour, use multiple sessions (for example, at 3:00AM, again at dawn, and then again at dusk).

The desire to meditate will continue to grow as the consciousness expands and positive results are seen in daily activities. The feeling of happiness and the sense of calm, in conjunction with improved physical and mental functions, will be an incentive to invest deeper in the practice. Be patient and trust the guidance that emerges from within. Trust the Truth that emerges from the expanded consciousness. Take time to reflect on personal choices, for each one is like a root that nourishes the tree to which it is connected—the tree of life, your life.

A poor diet, drugs, alcohol, stress, and insufficient rest will weaken the connection between the endocrine system and the Life Force. Nourishing the body is necessary to maintain the equilibrium between the body, mind, and the Life Force. Diet is directly related to the nature of the physical structure (human body) being built. The function of the endocrine and consequently its link with the Life Force will be weakened if the body is malnourished.

The body prepares for whatever is held within the mind. When an intention is held within the mind, it is manifested within the physical body. The subconscious prepares the body for whatever the mind intends, positive or negative. When the intention is personal change (healing through the correction of errors), the physical body prepares for this change. For example, food taken by the body will be directed to fortify the appropriate cells necessary to undertake the transformation.

Elements of the earth hold a potential which is either positive or negative. Food carries this potential. Certain foods will harmonize with the body. Foods contain properties necessary for healing the conditions that are common in the area where it is grown. For example, local foods contain properties that aid with the negative effects of pollution on the organs of the endocrine. Organically grown food will not only aid in cleansing the endocrine, but will also improve its functions.

Avoid foods grown in countries which experienced nuclear events. The food will contain properties necessary for neutralizing the effect of radiation in that part of the world, and if consumed by humans, will negatively impact the harmonics between the endocrine system and the Life Force.

Treat all food sources with honour and respect. Food provides the building blocks of physical life, with the potential to become cells of the human body. Similarly, respect the entire planet. What is now a table or chair was once perhaps the flesh of an animal or human being that was transformed by the earth. Decaying compost has the potential to one day be transformed into human flesh. Humans are part of the ecosystem of the planet.

After a period of two months, a balanced diet of local, organically-grown vegetables will cleanse the endocrine, restoring the equilibrium between the mind, body, and Life Force. Love and Truth will flow into the consciousness. The difference will be noticeable. Life will feel different after such a diet. Deeper meditations will be the result. Done in conjunction with physical adjustments, even deeper meditations will result. Healing will also result from correcting errors or changing the karmic patterns which are recognized during the state of silence when meditating. The result will be a new way of life created by the new patterns.

Sensitivity to self and others will grow. Powerful emotions will touch the deepest recesses of the soul. The world will feel like it is upside down where there is injustice, betrayal, and many forms of discord. Love will take on a different meaning where everyone will be accepted regardless of condition. Love will radiate from every cell of the body and through every thought in the mind. Love will be expressed as compassion. When asked, the heart will choose to give freely without expectations. Empathy for the disenfranchised will translate into kindness, charity, and imparting of hope. An attitude of thankfulness will fill the transformed consciousness, creating a state of happiness that will be felt all the way to the depths of the subconscious.

Part Twenty
Light

Light Which Defines Life

Take a moment to visualize the heart as the centre of physical life. The heart shines as it is embraced by the spark of light shining from "above" (a distant realm), radiating outward to touch the people and objects within its reach. As it is above, so shall it be here in the physical realm. In other words, light emanating from above possesses like potential when it shines within the hearts of humans here in the physical realm.

The blueprint held within the light determines what manifests here on the earth below. Heaven is a state of being which exists within the realm of light. This very light that shines from above, making its way into the physical realm as the source of life here on Earth. Manifesting the fullness of this light through the physical body is living in a heavenly state here on Earth. Love and Truth are forms of this light.

Take a moment to visualize heaven through the eyes of the imagination. Envision this light streaming from above, connecting with a heart where it can manifest as Love and Truth here on Earth. The desire for expression is the manifestation of the light within. Feel the desire emerging from within to manifest Love and Truth and thereby experience heaven here on Earth.

Take a moment to reflect on being in a heavenly state. Take a slow, deep breath and relax. Feel light emerging from within. Envision everything around you illuminated by light. Within a temporal existence here on Earth, know your life and all the life around you were born of this light. Know that each breath drawn into the body offers the opportunity to manifest light.

Take a moment to see and feel this light within the mind. Feel the Love emerging from the light within the heart. Feel the Truth emerging within the heart. Know that the expression of life is Love. Know that the expression of life is founded upon Truth. Know that the light within is Love and Truth. With the power vested within, grow the light to encompass those around you. Feel the Love which emanates from the heart expands to encompass the whole world.

All beings of light hold the power to radiate Love which touches every corner of the planet. Know that the spark of Love will fall on fertile ground. Many hearts will respond to the frequencies of Love and Truth as they are felt within. Imagine a world illuminated with this sparkling light shining through the hearts of all humankind.

Crown of Light

Choices made during each lifetime will result in physical and mental changes. The process of correcting errors and dissolving karma will disassemble the psyche and rebuild it on the platform of Love and Truth. In doing so, life will be different. Choices made today will determine the nature of life being built for the future. The future will be a time enlightened by the knowledge and experience collected on the journey there.

When making choices today, the wisdom of the knowledgeable future self would be invaluable. If it was possible to see into the future before making choices, or to step back for a moment and gather all the wisdom of the universe before embarking on any journey, life would be much simpler.

Each human life here on Earth was created by a spark of light. This is the spark which is shining within the human body, activating life. The complete blueprint of existence held within the light also shines within each human being. The wisdom that manifested human life in the physical world is also held within the spark.

Choices that were made by this creation determined the nature and current state of being. The mind of a child is a blank slate upon which experiences are written. Throughout a lifetime, the wisdom collected from experiences fill the slate of the mind.

The dynamics of physical existence, which was created by the manifestation of light, can be explored within the state of silence that occurs during meditation. Past, present and also future events will become visible. Wisdom held therein becomes accessible and can be used when making present-day choices.

One who is committed to fulfilling the purpose of life will use the wisdom of past, present and future to manifest only Love and Truth. In so doing, a heavenly state of being will result where the consciousness sparkles like a rainbow of light. The light within the consciousness fills the whole being (mind, body, and psyche) with indescribable happiness. With each choice that embraces Love and Truth, the light that emanates from within will grow in strength. It will first appear as a glow around the body, and a golden halo around the head. It can expand to embrace the whole world.

Part Twenty-One
On the Road to Victory

*"For whatsoever is born of God overcometh the world: and this is the **victory** that overcometh the world, even our faith." (1 John 5:4, Holy Bible, King James Version).*

The practice of meditation will prepare the mind for the challenges that will emerge when new situations are encountered during everyday experiences. Buried deep within the mind are patterns created by situations from the past. New situations may be faced with wisdom gathered from past experiences, by consulting others, or by resorting to patterns from the past. Following past patterns may feel like instinct or intuition. Each new situation is an opportunity to ignore external or internal influences and instead choose to apply Love and Truth.

Victory is the act of overcoming. A road is a pathway that leads to a conclusion. The pathway of life is filled with challenges to correct errors. Successfully correcting an error is one victory. The war will be won when all errors are corrected. The result will be indescribable happiness.

Each error that is corrected can be viewed as the removal of one faulty brick from the structure of the psyche. Choices that embrace Love and Truth will add new sturdy brick, rebuilding the psyche from the ground up on a new foundation. Balance is achieved by removing something and replacing it with something else. Victory is achieved by disassembling the psyche, removing errors, and rebuilding with Love and Truth. Being "born of God" is symbolism for the new psyche that is created by "overcoming the world" (correcting errors).

Love and Truth are forces that exist everywhere and touch everything. They touch every cell within the human body and can be felt in moments of silent contemplation. The journey of life is about aligning the psyche with them. This is the purpose for being here in this realm, and victory is achieving this purpose.

The mind is constantly undergoing change without being consciously aware that new ideas and perspectives are being assimilated. The human body is an amazing mechanism with the ability to adapt to its surroundings. Under the command of the Life Force, the body and mind will adjust in response to changes in the physical and mental environment. For example, the body has been gradually adjusting to an increasingly toxic atmosphere. Since this change is gradual, the mind is oblivious to what is occurring and accepts the new reality as normal. These changes are not only physical. For example, personality changes occur with the ever-shifting landscape of morals. The mind is blind to this occurrence. The environment and morals are just two examples. The integration of new technology, which then becomes a way of life, is another powerful example. Evolution may be an appropriate term for this process; physical and mental changes have been occurring since time immemorial.

Practising meditation is not simply musing or being quiet for an extended period. With dedication, it evolves into a lifestyle where time is systematically set aside to introspectively seek a connection to the true self—the source of Truth. Its purpose is to find the doorway that exposes the mechanics of the psyche. It is also about opening the door to the true nature of self. During the practice, patterns that define the psyche are set aside to expose the true self—a vantage point where the Spirit can observe the conscious and subconscious.

From this position, the Spirit can take hold of the rudder to navigate life in a new direction rather than following patterns established by the past. The journey onward will feel different, more positive, and calming. Instead of feeling like a boat being tossed about on stormy waters, it becomes a lifestyle which is filled with a sense of stability, direction, and purpose, much like a vessel being navigated through still waters.

The journey towards rebirth is a significant commitment and a sacrifice. It requires sacrificing the patterns which previously defined life. People, places, and things which do not contribute positively to the new and desired lifestyle must be abandoned. The new lifestyle will also have its challenges. For example, it is not normal to practice meditation on an airplane or bus. This is a challenge one will face when travelling at the time chosen to meditate. It will be the same if the time to practice rolls around when friends are visiting. It would have been better to arrange a time to allow for the practice. In order to honour the personal commitment to a new lifestyle, relationships with friends and family will change. These are two examples where difficult changes will be required while navigating through uncharted and tempestuous waters towards a new life.

Fear of change will be an ever-present deterrent. When fear knocks on the door using logic and reason to convince you to give up this new and challenging lifestyle and turn back to the old way, remember it is a commitment made out of Love to oneself. It is out of this Love that difficult choices must be made to reap the benefits of eternal joy.

Being committed to a new lifestyle requires implementing many difficult changes in everyday activities. Living the Truth will always involve challenging choices. Once the journey has progressed to this stage where errors are being corrected, the state of inner peace, happiness, and the feeling of accomplishment will overshadow the anguish caused by difficult changes. Victory will be the consolation. The apostle Paul sees this victory as "overcoming the world".

PART TWENTY-TWO
Meditate Upon the Light Within

Guided Imagery

One of the techniques used during meditation to create a state of calm is called "guided imagery". With this technique, the imagination is used to create images within the consciousness which activate the pineal, where melatonin is synthesized. Melatonin is a naturally occurring hormone generated by the pineal during sleep cycles. When it is released into the bloodstream, it creates a state of calm that lasts up to forty minutes.

Imagination involves the creation of images within the consciousness by protons, neutrons, and electrons interacting in the brain. The mind is aware that the images are not part of "physical reality" because of its source.

Reality within the physical world is also based on images that form in the consciousness. Science would explain that electrons, protons, and neutrons interact inside the brain to create the images within the consciousness. These images are the result of light being passed through the eyes, reflected on the retina, and transferred to the brain by the optic nerve. The mind then interprets the image and accepts it as a part of "physical reality."

Images that form in the brain, no matter the source, result from the same process: the interaction of electrons, protons, and neutrons. The difference between imagination and physical reality lies in the source of light. Imagination results from Spirit Light, whereas "physical reality" results from reflected earthly light (such as the sun, moon, or a light bulb) which enters the brain through the eyes of flesh. Whether the light emerges from the Spirit or reaches the brain through physical eyes, the resulting image inside the brain is the result of similar physics and chemistry. It is the mind that assesses the source of light using logic to determine whether the image is real or imagined.

Dreams are the result of a process similar to imagination. Instead, the light emerges from the Spirit in the form of images. The images are wrapped in emotions to form scenarios before being transmitted to the brain.

The physical response to images within the consciousness is the same regardless of source. For example, a state of calm would be created within the body and the mind when images such as a sunrise, calm waters of a lake, lush forests, or grassy meadows enter the consciousness. When used in conjunction with feelings, the result would be similar to dreams. The nature of the images and feelings will determine the type of reaction. This technique can be used during meditation to calm the body, mind, and consciousness.

Preparation

Meditations can be practised individually or in a group setting with a narrator. Beginners that find it difficult to still the mind will benefit from a group setting.

Find a quiet place that will remain undisturbed for a selected time period. Pre-dawn and sunrise meditations in a natural setting are conducive to achieving the state of silence.

Find a comfortable and relaxed position. Close your eyes. Take a deep breath and become aware of the physical senses. Observe the areas that feel disturbed and prepare to restore calm. Focus intently on each disturbance within the body and mind, and then let it go before moving on to the next. The objective is creating a space of inner silence.

Listen to the ambient sounds for a moment, then allow them to drift into the distance.

Focus on the nose as air rushes inward with each breath. Feel the sensation of the air as it enters the body. Allow the sensation of each breath to drift to the far corners of the mind.

Focus on the taste buds. Recall sensations of a delicious nourishing meal. Tantalize the taste buds by thinking of the most delicious fruit. Recall the feeling of being nourished. Allow this feeling to drift to the far reaches of the mind.

Focus on the surface of the skin and become aware of every cell. Start at the tip of your toes and move your awareness up through each part of your body—the soles of your feet, through your legs, into your lower torso and back, up through your chest and arms, down to your fingertips, through your neck, into your face, and out through your crown. Recall the most captivating sensations felt by the skin. Recall the feeling of cold negated by the warmth of a sweater or jacket. Think about textures that awakened the fingertips or a warm hand which transmitted feelings of caring or love. Reflect upon the richness of such physical abilities and be thankful in the moment for the opportunity to experience the sense of touch. Now, allow these thoughts and memories to drift to the farthest corners of the mind.

Focus on the sense of sight. Reflect upon images from past experiences which your brain interpreted as remarkable. Allow the mind to drift for a moment to places such as a beautiful ocean, lake, or perhaps daffodils dancing in the breeze around a peaceful pond. The mind may be awakened by the memory of a painting or the beauty radiating from a human face. Allow all these images to easily drift away into the distance.

Recall moments when the body's surrounding aura was disturbed—think of times, places, people, or incidents which caused hairs at the back of the neck or arms to stand on end. Perhaps it was a moment when you met someone for the first time. Focus on the sensation of having the aura disturbed. Hold the sensation for a moment, and then let it go.

As the senses become quiet, focus inward. Take a moment to listen and experience the silence. Within the place of silence, observe the presence of a light. Feel the energy of the light. It is a humbling presence.

Within the silence of the moment, feel the connection with this light as a source of inner power that illuminates the mind with thoughts and feelings. Feel the power of the light to direct life with Love and Truth.

Take a deep breath. Focus on the light. Feel it expand to fill the heart. Feel the flow of blood pumping through the veins, energizing every cell within the body with the light from the heart. Feel the light glistening from every energized cell. The entire body glows as the light expands outwards as far as the mind can travel.

As the body is energized with inner light, take a deep breath. Realize that what is being seen within the consciousness is from a place beyond the imagination. It is from the Life Force. It is from a place which offers only Truth. See this Truth as part of your life. Realize that the physical life, which emerges from the beat of the heart, is a manifestation of Truth.

As the Life Force connects with the mind, the consciousness expands to embrace all of reality. The consciousness is at one with all of existence. All of life is now enlightened by the light of the Life Force which flows from above into the heart.

Visualize the light flowing from above. Feel it as it enters the crown, activating the brain and flowing through the spine all the way to the feet and down to the earth below. Like a light bulb that illuminates when electricity flows through a circuit, the body glows when the circuit between the stars and the earth is completed.

Like a rainbow that emerges due to the prism effect as sunlight passes through the atmosphere, the light shining from above passes through the body and splits into all the colours of the rainbow. Each colour of light is a key that activates physical life. Three of these frequencies are located above the heart and three below. The nature of the light determines the nature of the physical being that is being animated. The nature of the light is a function of the Spirit. Realize this is the light that is felt during the practice of meditation.

Each light frequency or colour illuminates a different chakra in the body. Colour is vibration. Vibration results in movement. Movement is the source of change. Change is directed by choice.

The throat chakra, which centers on the thyroid, is activated by the blue frequency. It is the place of communication and self-expression. Feel the desire to express Truth strengthened by the light.

Feel the yellow light as it activates the solar plexus chakra in the area of the pancreas, the centre of empowerment and self-will. Anticipate the feeling of desire for self-determination empowered by free will to choose.

The third eye, the pineal chakra, is the place of perception and is activated by indigo. Feel the sense of awareness grow with clarity.

The frequency of orange light activates the sacral chakra, the source of creativity. Feel the urge from within to innovate and build.

The purple light, which activates the pituitary gland, is associated with the crown chakra. Feel the connection with the Life Force, the centre of self-advancement, enlightenment, silence, and indescribable happiness.

The root chakra is activated by red light. It is associated with the gonads. It is the area of survivability. In conjunction with the third chakra, it activates fight or flight responses. Anticipate feelings of well-being, safety, and belonging.

The colour green is associated with the heart chakra. This light frequency activates the thymus gland which radiates Love. All of life's intentions, whether they emerge from the upper three or lower three chakras can flow through the heart, where there is an innate desire to manifest Love. Empowered by the self-will of the third chakra, they can all be filtered with Love so the feelings that emerge from the heart chakra are compassion and forgiveness.

Take a moment to visualize the beauty of an enlightened life: light travelling from a distant realm, passing through the physical body, illuminating it with all the colours of the rainbow, and flowing down into the earth below the feet.

For a moment, travel back in time and imagine the brilliant light gathering physical cells in order to manifest your life through the process of physical birth here on Earth.

Visualize your existence as a series of moments that are opportunities to manifest thoughts and ideas like seeds within the mind. These are the seeds that have grown into the life being lived in this moment.

Realize that each moment is an opportunity to manifest the energy of Love within. Realize this light can grow to embrace the whole world.

Imagine for a moment the amazing and glorious opportunity each breath offers to manifest, within the physical realm, thoughts and desires which originate from the Spirit as its light shines here in the physical realm through your physical body.

Embrace the opportunity to shine as an enlightened being, manifesting the light of Love and Truth in all its brilliance, here on Earth.

Take a deep breath and embrace it all. Reflect on the experience for five minutes.

As the time approaches to stop meditating, take a moment to recall the feelings that were experienced during the practice. Determine how they can be used to manifest Love and Truth during everyday experiences.

When you are ready, take a deep breath. As you exhale, slowly bring your consciousness back to the physical body and its surroundings. Gently open your eyes.

Following each meditation, take a moment to examine your thoughts and feelings. Then, record the experiences in your journal.

Prayer of Bliss

Divine Creator of Life
Divine Guardian of Life
Divine Angels
Divine Teachers
Divine Guides
All that offer Love and Truth

It is my prayer that you would be with me
That you would guide me
That you would protect me
That you would council me

Embrace me that I may feel Loved
Guide me that I may find my way
Protect me from all that seek to take me away from my sacred path
Council me to embrace Truth

Help me to always see and manifest my Divinity
Help me to transcend the way of the World
Help me to be who I am, Spirit clothed in Flesh
Help me to shine with Love and Truth, always
Teach me to be all that I am as an example of Love and Truth
Teach me to manifest my Divinity that I may find Bliss
Teach me to transcend the way of the mind and embrace Truth

Teach me to embrace Love as the deliverer from my past actions
Help me transcend the controls of the mind and become who I am
Help me to become all that I am, Spirit in command of my life
Help me to transform my life and embrace the Light of my Spirit which is Bliss
Amen

Pray not for the world, but for yourself, and when your prayer is answered and the Light you shine is the brilliance of your Spirit, it will illuminate the world around you with Love and Truth and Peace. Prepare to meditate with an attitude of prayerfulness. Amen.

PART TWENTY-THREE
Crystal Light Meditation

Preparation

The objective of this meditation is achieving a state of oneness with the Life Force. Balancing the energy centers within the human body will restore the flow of energy between the physical body and the Life Force. Healing of mental and physical conditions which result in an imbalance will be initiated. When balance is restored, the consciousness will enter into a state of calm. The desire to manifest Love and Truth will be felt from within. The consciousness will be filled with unimaginable feelings of peace and joy.

Guided imagery will be used to examine each energy centre and reveal imbalances. It will start at the root and progress to the crown. The process will be similar for each chakra, and the mind will find it repetitive.

Each chakra is unique and the process of finding balance will also be unique.

It is not necessary to address all the chakras in each session. Studying your journal may reveal specific chakras that need attention. In the earlier example where the past was hidden out of fear of judgement, corrections can be addressed by choosing to filter the energy through the heart chakra, the centre of Love. Perfect Love holds the power to dissolve fear. Truth holds the power to manifest choice. Since the imbalance emerged from the first chakra, the source of fear, the third, fourth and fifth chakras will be involved in correcting the error. The will to change emerges from third. Manifesting Truth emerges from the fourth. Filtering intentions through the fourth chakra is the process of injecting Love into the situation.

Allow sufficient time to experience the entire meditation. Start with three minutes for each energy centre and thirty minutes for the entire session. This can be increased in succeeding sessions. Use a timer to alert the mind to when it is time to end the session. The desire to remain in the state of calm being experienced during the practice will be strong. Make a commitment to return to physical consciousness when signalled at the end of the session.

Crystal Light Meditation

Take a moment to settle into a comfortable and relaxed posture. With eyes gently closed, inhale deeply. Slowly exhale. Prepare to leave the physical world behind and explore a vast realm which can only be reached using the powers of the mind.

Visualize a tree providing shade beside a lake. Flowers of every colour sway gently in the breeze, surrounding the water that glistens in the sunlight. Imagine standing on a flat, warm rock at the water's edge; feel the pure clear water lap gently against the rock. The water feels warm and kind. Realize that water in all its forms acts as a conduit that connects everything. With the touch of the water, feel the connection with everything. Feel the connection where water is the foundation of all life on Earth. Feel the connection with everything on the planet.

Take a moment to bathe in the reflection of the shimmering water. Feel the shimmering light fill the consciousness. The light within grows brighter. Imagine the water becoming perfectly still. Imagine touching the water and connecting the mind, body, and Spirit with everything here on Earth.

Take a gentle but deep breath and allow light to fill the consciousness. Allow the body to feel lighter and the mind to grow silent. Listen to the silence. Feel the joy emerge from the depths of the light. Imagine walking forward, upon the surface of the water, to a place in the distance—beyond the shore across the lake. There, among the lush foliage and flower gardens, lies a crystalline structure. Seven levels are visible. A crystal path leads to a door.

Envision the door being open. Walk through the door. Feel the warm floor energizing the feet. The room is filled with a gentle glow. White light streams through a red crystal suspended from the ceiling's centre; it radiates a warm, calm, red glow. Permit yourself to be overcome by a feeling of peace. Imagine the light flowing down through your feet and into the earth below. Know that you are supported by and united with the earth. Experience a feeling of gratitude. Thoughts for reflection are survivability, well-being, and safety. Give thanks for the gift of abundance. Rest in the healing power of the light.

Visualize moving to the next level of the crystalline structure. Light shines through an orange crystal suspended in the middle of the room. A gentle glow fills the room. Stand under the crystal, allowing the orange glow to bathe your whole body. Receive the energy from the light. Allow it to fill your body. The centre of creativity is activated. Feel the desire to be productive. Become aware of its purpose and its ability to manifest the intention of the light—to create, here in this realm, an environment underlined by Love. The earth below provides cells that are energized by the Light from above. The Spirit provides the intention to be manifested by the body using its creative power guided by the mind. Ponder all the possibilities offered by the fertile ground of the mind. Thoughts for reflection are emotions, creativity, and temptation. Rest for a time in the healing power of the Light.

Visualize moving onward and upward to the third level. The floor is warm and crystalline. Light streaming from above shines through a yellow crystal suspended within the room. Feel the gentle glow that fills the room. Stand under the crystal and bath in the yellow glow. Feel the dance of every cell within as they resonate with the Light. Feel the strength of will being harnessed and fortified. Know from within the depths of your being that the strength to manifest the desires of the Spirit grows as the resonance of the yellow Light harmonizes with the cells of the physical body. Relax. Breathe in the yellow light, allowing it to energize the cells within. Feel the strength of will growing stronger with the healing and cleansing power of the yellow Light. Feel the self being empowered to choose a path of evolution and creativity. Thoughts for reflection are courage, power, self-will, and empowerment. Rest for a time as the body bathes in the healing power of the Light.

Visualize moving onward and upward to the fourth level. The floor is crystalline and glowing with the energy of the yellow crystal from the level below. The Light streaming from above is shining through a green crystal suspended in the middle of the room. A gentle green glow fills the room. Stand under the crystal and bathe in its green Light. Feel the dance of every cell within as they resonate in unison with the Light. The mind becomes aware of a doorway between the Spiritual and physical realms. The consciousness is filled with Love flowing from above. What lies above in the realm of the Spirit shines through to the physical below. The heavenly realms will thereby be manifested through your body. As it is above, through the doorway of the heart, so shall it be below. As the light flows downward to the levels below, the energy of the yellow Light empowers the body. The energy of the orange Light offers creative direction. The energy from the red Light offers the instrument which can manifest the desires of that creativity. Choice is the directing force. With the power to choose (self-empowerment), the Light from the heart area can be directed where it is needed to influence all the facets of life below. Thus, Love, which is the manifesting energy of the green light, can be chosen as the filter when dealing with all aspects of life in the physical realm. Thoughts to ponder are healing, compassion, and the transforming power of Love. Bathed in the energy of the green light, the body rests for a time, absorbing the Truth being shared.

Visualize moving onward and upward to the fifth level. The warm crystalline floor is glowing with the energy of the green crystal from the level below. The brilliant white light streaming from above shines through a blue crystal suspended within the room. A gentle glow of blue fills the room. Standing under the crystal, the body is bathed with this energy. The power within to manifest the very essence of the Spirit is activated by the Light. As the body resonates with the blue energy, the desire to manifest Truth becomes resolute. The power of the voice to manifest the Truth of the Spirit is fortified. Communication between the chakras is strengthened. The glow of the green emanating from the heart filters intentions so that Truth may be manifested with Love. The thoughts to ponder are communication and self-expression. Bathed in the healing power of the blue Light, the body rests for a time.

Visualize moving upward to the sixth level of the crystalline structure. The warm crystalline floor is glowing with the blue energy from below. The pure white Light is streaming from above. It shines through an indigo crystal suspended in the room. A gentle indigo glow fills the room. Stand under the crystal and bathe within the indigo energy. Awareness expands to embrace the physical and Spiritual realms. A doorway to the past, present, and future opens, revealing Truth held within the soul and the psyche. Intuition is awakened. The ancients describe the activation of this awareness as the opening of the third eye. The awareness of the desires of the Spirit fills the consciousness. Filtered by the green energy of Love, this awareness flows down the body to be manifested by the power of the blue energy. The Light travels up and down through every energy centre as all work in harmony with each other. The eyes of the Spirit are opened, offering insight. Thoughts to ponder are intuition and calm. Bathed in the healing power of the indigo Light, the body rests for a time.

Visualize moving upward to the seventh level. The warm crystalline floor is glowing with an indigo hue from below. A pure and brilliant white Light is streaming from above. It shines through a purple crystal suspended from the ceiling. A gentle purple glow fills the room. Standing under the crystal on a floor glowing with indigo energy, the body is flooded with the purple energy. The Light travels up and down through every energy centre of your body as all work in harmony with each other. Every cell within the physical body shines as they resonate with the frequency of the purple Light. Within this Light, the body grows lighter and the feeling of weightlessness ensues. With eyes closed, the consciousness is filled with the sensation that the body is floating above the indigo, crystalline floor. Bathed in the purple Light, the body rests for a time. Thoughts to ponder are indescribable happiness, balance, and evolution. Choose to manifest the purple energy through each chakra, all the way down. As the whole being resonates with the purple energy, indescribable joy floods into the consciousness. Remain bathed in purple Light until alerted by the alarm that it is time to return to physical consciousness.

Take a deep and gentle breath, exhale, relax, and prepare to leave the crystalline sanctuary. Visualize walking down the stairs to the entrance. Calmly walk towards the glistening body of water. Feeling lighter than air, slowly walk across the water and return to the place surrounded by dancing lilies. Relax, breathe, slowly exhale, and allow the eyes to open softly. Become aware of the environment as you return to physical consciousness. Take a moment to feel the sensations that the physical body has retained from the experience. Take a moment to feel and be in the indescribable happiness and sense of balance.

Reflection

The water being walked upon symbolizes the pathway opened by meditation. The crystalline structure represents the Life Force within. Imagery used during this meditation is only an example. When practicing meditation, choose imagery that is personal and inspires peace and calm. Visiting a sacred place, walking in the park, listening to a babbling brook, gazing at the blue sky, sitting under a shady tree, listening to calming music, recalling moments of happiness, and being with an inspirational teacher are a few examples.

Using the imagery of crystals may offer new realizations during the session, immediately after, from dreams, or any time in the future. These realizations would appear as awareness within the consciousness in the form of a new or different perspective. It may be related to the self, another person, or a situation. For example, the one who hid the truth in a relationship may become aware of a deep sense of shame, guilt, the hurt being caused, or the unstable ground upon which the relationship was built. Each perspective or awareness is connected to one or more chakras. If there is an imbalance, the energy will not flow freely, obscuring the purpose of the chakra. For example, the desire to manifest Truth will become obscured.

One of the lessons the practice of meditation offers is the role of balance in one's life. In the physical world, every action results in a reaction. For example, overeating results in excess weight which, over time, can lead to other more serious health conditions, such as diabetes, heart problems, and obesity.

Sir Isaac Newton (1642-1726), the well-known scientist, stated, "For every action or force in nature there is an equal and opposite reaction". For example, the force generated in an internal combustion engine is transferred to the wheels of a vehicle enabling it to move at high speeds. Similarly, the backward thrust from a jet engine pushes the airplane forward at even higher speeds.

The role of "balance" in our lives is similar, except it transcends physical bounds. King Solomon wrote, *"A soft answer turneth away wrath: but grievous words stir up anger." (Proverbs 15:1, Holy Bible, King James Version)*. The expression of Love (a soft answer) will always return Love, even if the result is not immediate. An expression of Truth will unbind conditions that resulted from hiding the truth, restructuring the dynamics within the relationship. A life built upon Truth is destined for the indescribable happiness which manifests when there is balance.

Each chakra is connected to a different part of our humanity. Starting from the root chakra and moving upwards, the feelings are related to survivability, creativity, empowerment and free will, love, truth, awareness and insight, and indescribable happiness. Balancing the chakras is achieved by synchronizing feelings with the nature of the chakras.

Unfiltered by errors, the Life Force will illuminate the chakras in all their brilliance. There is a unique feeling associated with each chakra. However, imbalance will restrict the flow of light, changing the resonance of the chakra and the feeling within the consciousness. For example, feelings related to survivability or well-being can change to fear or greed. Creativity can change to self-destruction. Empowerment can change to fear and self-denial. Love can change to fear or hate. Truth can change to fear and denial. Awareness can change to doubt. Denial of the Life Force will result in guilt, anger, and sadness.

The feelings and emotions experienced when practicing the *Crystal Light Meditation* are real. If happiness is felt, it is real and will remain for a period of time. Remember the feeling. Choose to navigate life to a place where this happiness becomes the permanent state of the consciousness. Dedicate time each day to visit the crystal sanctuary. Walk across the still waters to reconnect with the enlightened self. View this place as a home where the Spirit can find rest, one which is eternal and always filled with joy.

At the end of the practice, take time to reflect on the experience. Examine the consciousness and feelings to determine what is different within. Realize that you will feel different because Truth and Love were experienced. All that you have felt, seen and learnt will result in change. Reflect upon the parts of life which can benefit from all you have learnt. Determine where Love and Truth can be injected into daily experiences in order to manifest the change you desire. Love and Truth can be viewed as the North Star that offers guidance to the place of balance.

In the case where the partner hid the truth, the error was exposed to the consciousness while meditating. The awareness within the consciousness resulted in a different choice, one based on Love and Truth instead of fear. The bond between the two grew stronger, building on a foundation of mutual acceptance.

In the case where the inheritance was stolen from the younger brother, the practice of meditation strengthened his resolve, taking away the anger and disappointment, replacing the negativity with unconditional acceptance.

Lessons can be learnt from the experiences of others who become teachers in the truest sense by demonstrating the application of Love and Truth in their lives.

Finally, before moving on to worldly tasks, spend time with your journal, recording the experiences you have encountered.

Questions

The practice of meditation will stimulate the inquiring mind, resulting in a quest for answers about life. Questions regarding life here on Earth and beyond will enter the mind. Do not accept the words written in this book as rote. Accept what emerges from within, and if the words in this book resonate with your Spirit, they can be accepted as your Truth also. Realize that Truth is eternal and belongs to everyone.

The Nature of Life

When encountering experiences that emerge due to the practice of meditation, questions regarding the genesis of life and the nature of the enlightened being will fill the inquiring mind. What is the Spirit or the Life Force and where did it come from? Can the mind understand the concept of physical birth, life and death, and their relationship with totality? Is totality simply defined as everything in existence? How can the mind understand the relationship between life on the planet, the indwelling Spirit, and totality?

Science does not offer the answer. It cannot explain everything. Gravity, for example, is an invisible force which impacts every atom on the planet and cannot be fully explained by scientists. It can be measured, but not fully explained. The force which animates human life on this planet is part of totality and is also invisible. Therefore, each living human being on the planet is an example of an unexplainable phenomenon.

During meditation, the mind is enlightened by the consciousness of the Spirit. This mind becomes aware that the human body is a vehicle which was created to experience the physical realm. The body was formed from physical cells that were attracted to each other by the magnetic nature of the Spirit. The body was designed to manifest the desires of the Spirit. Its functions are controlled by the brain. The brain is directed by both the mind and the Spirit. The mind is an independent entity with a connection to the Spirit. The mind is responsible for the functions of physical life, and while the Spirit holds the power to direct the mind, the mind has the free will to choose.

A bridge between the conscious mind and the Spirit is formed by thoughts and desires encased within feelings and emotions. Spirit communicates with the mind via this bridge.

Beyond the boundaries of the conscious mind lies the vast region of the subconscious, a landscape that can be viewed as totality. Both the conscious and subconscious impact human life.

The mind functions within the boundaries of the conscious. Dreams and visions offer a broader perspective of totality, as they access the entire landscape of conscious and subconscious. The language they use for communication is similar. Symbols encased within emotions are implanted within the consciousness and reflected upon the mind. Dreams occur during the sleep state, while visions can occur during meditation or at any other time.

Experiences in physical life originate from either carnal or Spiritual desires. An examination of the emotions connected with each desire will reveal its source—either Love or fear. Love originates from the Spirit while fear is a creation of the mind based on the individual's ego. This dual nature of physical existence is the result of the desires of the Spirit in conflict with the functioning of the mind. The freedom to choose which desire to manifest determines one's current state of being and the direction life will ultimately take.

The free will to choose is a function of the mind and the navigator of life. Happiness results when choice is aligned with the nature of the Spirit. This form of happiness is eternal. As a component of life, the mind is also eternal. The impact of choice on the mind is eternal. Consequently, when the clothing of clay is shed, a unique soul remains. The name given to the human remains attached to the soul. This is the case for each sojourn on the physical realm. When a soul is impacted by fear, it will perpetually cycle through birth, life, and death in an attempt to correct mistakes or errors. This perpetual cycling will end when the laws of karma are fulfilled.

The approach to life experiences, according to the law of karma, should always be one of acceptance, forgiveness, and repair.

An understanding of the building blocks of life will offer an insight into the nature and history of the knowledge pertaining to the indwelling Spirit. This knowledge becomes an aid when contemplating current life situations and can be used as a stepping stone into the future. For instance, it can help to overcome thoughts regarding the repetition of negative patterns or the seeking of recompense, which not only serve as stumbling blocks, but create karmic ties.

The rainbow is a metaphor for life. It has been appearing in the sky since time immemorial and can be interpreted as a symbol of the link between physical body and Spirit. In a similar way, as the light of the Spirit shines into the physical realm, it splits into rays of energy in a rainbow of colour. Each colour resonates with one of the seven glands of the endocrine.

Each life here on Earth can enact the laws of karma to deconstruct its mental framework and permanently detach its light from this realm. In other words, the body, mind, and Spirit are linked together here on Earth and the laws of karma can open the door to free the Spirit from this realm forever.

Ties to the physical realm are the result of choices which navigated life to situations currently being experienced. The physical reality currently in existence emerged out of the collective choices of humanity. The direction the world is heading is impacted by collective choice. Many minds remain oblivious as the physical realm obscures the Truth, much like rose-coloured glasses do. These filters result in focusing on day-to-day events and personal challenges, and lead to a numbing of the power of Love that emerges from the fourth chakra. The filters have changed the perception of the rainbow in the sky as well as the nature of Spirit light as it resonates with human life. Errors from the past colour the perception of reality and result in choices which create karmic ties to this realm. In other words, spending each day in an environment that obscures the true colour of reality will impact the quality of personal life and, subsequently, much of society.

Meditation, dreams, and dissolving errors offer opportunities to view reality from a vantage point unobstructed by filters. The window through which life is perceived is unique to each person. Hope, love, fear, peace, patience, creativity, acceptance, and truth are filters through which the world can be perceived. The rose-coloured hue will be lifted to reveal only Truth.

With each error, a fragment of the Spirit separates from the whole, and is lost somewhere in darkness. These fragments are often replaced by aspects of fear. And like a disease, fear has the potential to taint the whole. Fragments have been scattered throughout reality as the Spirit journeyed through time. With each lost fragment, the Spirit is minimized or shrinks, thereby reducing the ability to experience the fullness of happiness.

Meditation holds the potential to rekindle the inner light and stoke it to full potential by reassembling the fragmented parts to become whole once more. Retrieving all lost fragments is pivotal in achieving the state of happiness.

On this journey, one must realize that happiness and enlightenment are different. Enlightenment is the ability to see through the eyes of the Spirit and focus on Love and Truth, while happiness is a state of consciousness where the Spirit, mind, and body manifest the Love and Truth that emerges from within. When life is navigated along the path underlined by Love and Truth, enlightenment is achieved on the way to the pinnacle of existence, which is the true state of happiness.

Faith

Consider faith. Typically, the word faith is used in conjunction with religious dogma. When applied, it results in a mental framework bound by non-evidential paradigms. Often these are based on the misinterpretations of religious doctrine.

Like Love and Truth, there are different perspectives on faith. Faith can be viewed as acceptance of a paradigm without validation. It results from an awareness that cannot be verified by scientific methods. Applying such faith results in action based on non-evidential belief.

As discussed earlier, faith can also refer to the acceptance of the non-evidential existence of an indwelling Life Force or Spirit, which is responsible for animating the physical body. In this case, applying faith relates to the understanding of inner guidance and using it in conjunction with the free will for self-determination.

The successful practice of meditation is dependent upon faith in oneself and the existence of an indwelling Life Force.

The Unknown Question

The practice of meditation will result in questions unique to each person. These questions are inherent to life, and we are always pursuing the answers. Words like ambition, aspiration, motivation, determination, initiative, instinct, eagerness, passion, and keenness all relate to this phenomenon. The mind, however, is not aware that it is seeking answers. Questions are simply part of its underlying structure or programming, which came into being upon inception into existence and is common to everyone. It defines who we are as individuals. The mind is a complex and independent entity created in the image of its creator. It is a spark (or child) which carries a copy of the blueprint from the light which created it, and within its underlying structure lies these questions.

The spark sought expression on the earth and found it in physical form. In so doing, it parted ways with the light from which it emerged, weakening the connection between the two. Free will navigates the spark in a different direction, away from its source programming, blueprint, or original nature, but questions remain within the fabric of its existence.

When the spark first entered the garden of the earth, its life was in total balance. The connection with its source remained strong and all the answers were known. History describes the vast changes that have occurred through time. The desire to experience the different aspects of this realm resulted in many changes. The spark grew further and further away from its true nature, eventually losing its direction and purpose. It became entangled within the realms of physical thought, losing its connection with its true nature. It lost its connection with the memories of its true nature as a being of light.

The earth's garden, fabled as Eden in the *Book of Genesis* in the *Holy Bible*, became a playground to conquer, ravage, and abuse; ultimately, its original nature was destroyed by this process. History books have recorded the wars, famine, domination, and slavery which resulted.

Fast forward to the present day and observe the state of the world where the "forces of good" and the "forces of evil" can be seen embedded within society. The unknown questions have resulted in an unconscious void which is being exploited by the "forces of evil" using "fear". Fear is one of the main weapons being used to influence change. Many of the western religions, teachings, and social norms that are emerging are shifting the psyche away from inner trust and guidance to methodologies based on societal slavery.

ABOUT MEDITATION

In the beginning, the first thought was borne from Love and carried within a crucible of Truth. Today, the true meaning of Love and Truth have been lost to most. Life continues within a blindness of false hope, and within this hope, lie tainted perceptions of Love and Truth. Deep within, however, the elements of light exist. If one is willing to search, the true essence of life will emerge.

The power still lies deep within each individual to grow both Love and Truth so they blossom into mighty oaks. In so doing, life on the planet can return to the original state of the fabled garden of Eden. It would once again be a place where Love and Truth manifest in balance with the creator of flesh, the earth. The mind still holds the power to direct an existence underlined by Love and Truth.

The mind's true nature lies within unanswered and unrealized questions: Who am I and what am I? Why am I here and where do I go from here? How do I get there? The answers lie in a place deeper than the most minute atom of physical life; they are held within the spark of light from which they were created. The blueprint of the Life Force which is embedded deep within.

The first thought that emerged from the parent light is: *"I AM" (Exodus 3:14, Holy Bible, King James Version)*. The spark that entered the earth realm carried the identical thought deep within its core. This thought also carried the answers to the unrealized questions.

The answers will indicate that life is evolving into a journey of discovery. What does this answer mean? Who and what is the *"I AM?"* How does one manifest the *"I AM"*?

The Answer

The expression of the Life Force is in the form of light. Thought is a manifestation of this light. It is the expression of thought that resulted in creation. Light was reflected through thought as the imagination of the Life Force. The mind of physical beings views this imagination as reality.

The spark of light, which fragmented from its source and entered the physical realm, experienced existence within the imagination of the Life Force. Carried within the spark is the original thought of the Life Force. This thought lies within the subconscious and forms the foundation of the mind. Within the fertile ground of the mind, questions emerge. The unknown questions originated from thought which was propelled into this physical realm and is now the seed of human purpose.

The first thought that lies at the core of the Life Force is *"I AM"*. The realization that questions emerge from this thought that lies deep within the mind sets the stage for the birth of intention. Intention can be in the form of a mission statement such as "I will be all that *I AM*". In other words, "*I AM*; therefore, I will be all that *I AM*". Within the state of silence which occurs during meditation, intentions are revealed and traced to the point of their inception.

Intention creates purpose. During the state of silence when meditating, purpose can be examined, understood, and consequently employed to navigate life in a desired direction.

Provided the seeds are nourished by Love and Truth, life will be navigated towards the original state which existed in the beginning, the place where the Spirit and the flesh existed in harmony with Love and Truth. It is a place that can be viewed as the fabled Garden of Eden, an environment of absolute abundance.

In the fabled garden, balance was maintained between the physical and spiritual with the expression of Love and Truth. Peace and happiness bloomed.

The return to this place would denote the end of a long journey. The end therefore is the beginning, and the beginning is the end.

Manifesting Light

The Garden of Eden does not exist anywhere on the planet today. The departure from the garden resulted from the loss of a conscious connection with the true nature of the light. This changed the mental landscape of humanity, and consequently, the trajectory of life on the planet. Over millions of years, the surface of the earth was reshaped in conjunction with the mental landscape of humanity.

Through time, physical human characteristics such as height, hair, facial features, and pigmentation have evolved as humans adapted to their natural environments.

Scientists have observed that flora and fauna are slowly disappearing. Many cities have become concrete jungles. Industries are destroying the natural rhythm of the planet by poisoning the water and polluting the air. Some people live in the shadow of tall buildings without any exposure to sunlight. Places that were once lush are now desert, unable to produce food to sustain physical life. Poverty and famine are emerging as the result.

The nomadic nature of humankind resulted from a distant past when survival was dependent upon weather and food source. Ingrained within the subconscious today is the need to relocate to environments which are more conducive to survival. Job, food, medicine, safety, and standard of living are a few of the reasons. This underlying nature resulted in a cornucopia of cosmopolitan societies. Many countries are becoming a melting pot of values influenced by education, language, race, belief systems, political affiliation, health, and wealth. Governments that continue to ignore global inequalities are becoming subject to social implosion.

The solution does not lie within a government or a monarchy. It is incumbent upon every human being to realize that the Life Force which animates the body, no matter the evolutionary path, remains the same for everyone. Physical differences do not impact the ability to manifest the light of the Spirit. Belief systems may differ; histories may differ; social and economic situations may differ. However, all of these do not change one simple Truth: every human life is capable of fully manifesting the light of the Spirit, as it was in the beginning. The playing field is equal for everyone, as the light which animates human life here on Earth is from one source. Everyone, regardless of origin, is designed with the same potential.

Peace is a function of Love. The path to peace in the world starts within. It starts with the element of Love which can be found within. This means looking beyond physical, economic, social, or moral differences to recognize and honour the light of the Life Force which animates life. It also means recognizing that the seed to become "all that *I AM*" lies within everyone.

This light which carries this seed or blueprint, holds the potential to Love without condition or expectation. The potential to manifest the light from within the heart exists in everyone.

Manifesting this light is a journey where every expression in life is underlined by Love. This simple act will once again restore the Eden concept here on Earth, a place where happiness will be recognized as the only commodity of value. Experiences such as enlightenment, miracles, and wisdom will simply be signposts along the path. The spiritual landscape will change, nullifying the laws of karma. Rebirth will be dictated only by choice. The *"I AM"* seed will blossom and the natural state of the Spirit will be restored. *"I AM ALL THAN I AM"* will become the personification of happiness.

Freedom

Manifesting the *"I AM"* is the essence of freedom. What is the difference between being truly free and being a subject of societal slavery?

When usage of time is not dictated by external sources such as a job or household tasks, many have lost the ability to navigate life during moments of aloneness. When the freedom to control personal time and determine self-direction is given away to a daily routine, being alone with nothing to do, which should be normal and natural, feels foreign. The awareness of this state of freedom has been lost or weaned out for many in today's society. Instead of being taught how to honour free will and personal desires, life has been designed from childhood to yield to the ways and directions of external sources, such as jobs, parents, church, and governments. Furthermore, some have been taught to ignore personal feelings for the greater good of a system, family, religion, or society.

Every child should be taught about personal power and self-determination. Every individual should be taught how to recognize and harness free will and the power to choose. Every individual should be taught how to recognize the Life Force within and how to define a life which honours its nature as the first and foremost commandment.

Savouring the essence of life that emerges from within should be the defining paradigm. The desire to experience and feel must emerge from within, not from external influences such as the experiences and feelings of others. For example, a desire from within may lead one to wake up each day to enjoy the sunrise, to immerse oneself in a crimson sunset, to walk under a moonlit sky, feeling the glory of a star-filled cosmos, and to sit silently beside a calm lake, are all moments to savour.

These are ways to experience the indwelling Spirit and feel the natural states of silence and happiness. In other words, expressing the light which shines within will result in true happiness.

One can be rich and experience true happiness. One can be poor and experience true happiness. One can be alone and experience true happiness. One can be in a crowd, cohabiting, or part of a family and experience true happiness.

These experiences are authentic only if the desire emerges from within one's own being. These are the experiences that make life feel complete. Everything else, such as jobs and household tasks, should be chosen solely to sustain the defining purpose which emerges from the depths of the Spirit within. True freedom lies in the capacity to recognize the power of the free will within and the ability to use it for self-direction in life. True freedom lies in experiencing the fullness of life by choosing self-determination in each and every moment.

Moments

The experiences that were planned for this incarnation are not only about creating the feelings that exist within a single moment in the present. This single moment resulted from choices which navigated life to the present. The moments that created experiences throughout the past are as important as the present moment. Collectively, these moments form a roadmap that leads to life in the present. The present moment holds the power to navigate and change direction, while the moments from the past serve only as wisdom. The intention of each incarnation is contained within the collection of all of these moments. The experiences held within them led to the present state of being. If each moment is the result of careful navigation using meditative guidance, the goal of the incarnation can be achieved in a single lifetime. It will lead to a present, that is a moment in the eyes of eternity, embraced by happiness.

Mastery of Life

During moments of reflection, remember that the water being walked upon symbolizes the pathway opened by meditation and the crystalline structure represents the Life Force within. The chart in

Appendix A represents the whole being, the Life Force in conjunction with the physical manifestation. Embracing the way of the Life Force here on Earth is the journey a master undertakes. Viewed as complicated, difficult, and unattainable, mastery is a simple process that everyone can follow to achieve the full potential of human existence.

Free will bestows power to navigate life back to its original state, as it was in the beginning. Light streaming from above passes through the crown and flows through the body, down into the earth, and like an electrical circuit, illuminates every cell within the human body. This Light is the source of life here on Earth. The essence of this Light is Love and Truth. Thus, the true nature of physical life is Love and Truth.

The Light from above, which enters the crown, passes through the Spirit. The souls associated with the Spirit act like a filter that changes the nature of the Light that passes through it. This filtered Light, which enlivens the human body, defines the unique nature of the human life which it manifests.

The nature of the Spirit is the result of choices made during its journey through time. This free will to choose resulted in the current nature of the Spirit. The same free will holds the power to restore the Spirit to its original state by making different choices. "The Book of Errors" contains the source code of the soul, which is to be rewritten as "On the Road to Victory", so that Love and Truth can shine through the cells of the body, unimpeded by filters. Mastery is achieved when Love and Truth flow from above, unfiltered, through the cells of the physical body.

The journey of a master is not contingent upon the power of free will to navigate life. Filters created in the past (karma) have been cleared. Only Love and Truth flow from above, enlivening and enlightening the physical being.

Part Twenty-Four
On Being a Master

Traditionally, the word "master" pertains to expertise in specific subjects. For example, one can master a musical instrument or an area of study and become an authority in the field, such as a master of science, theology, archaeology, or music. The art of self-defence, such as judo or karate, can also be mastered. The word "master" is also used as a sign of respect. During certain times in history, slaves would address their owner as "master", demonstrating respect, but it was out of fear. In ancient times, the word "master" had a different meaning. It referred to the ability to command all aspects of one's life.

The mastery of life, or self-mastery, goes beyond physical prowess to include the non-physical. It is achieved when all errors are corrected and karmic patterns from all lifetimes are dissolved. When this occurs, the expressions of the body, mind, consciousness, and psyche all operate in unison with the Life Force.

A master commands all aspects of the physical and non-physical self. Great dedication is required to reach this state. It goes beyond the level of practice one would invest in a temporal task, such as mastering a musical instrument like the piano. Mastering the self requires sacrificing the current state of being, which is defined both by Love and Truth, but also the errors from the past. On the path to self-mastery, the way of life and state of being will change as the parts defined by errors are removed. It will be viewed as sacrificing one's life by those who are not familiar with the process.

The practice of meditation will open the door to self-mastery. Dedication to the practice will present opportunities for dissolving karma. Correcting the errors of the past will restore life according to the blueprint of the Life Force. It requires an open channel between the Life Force and the mind. This is the channel which opens during the state of silence when meditating.

When errors exist that cannot be corrected within the current lifetime, multiple lifetimes will be required. Self-mastery is achieved with commitment and dedication which transcends a single lifetime. All aspects of life must be dedicated to the single goal of becoming a master. Nothing else can be more important. The challenges will be the most difficult ones a person will ever face, as it involves overcoming the resistance which the mind will present. It means sacrificing the current and familiar way of being for a different and unknown framework.

To achieve self-mastery, the practice of meditation must become part of every aspect of life. For example, each meal must begin and end with meditation; each activity must begin with meditation. All aspects of life must be approached from a meditative state—where the mind and body are united as one with the Spirit. The Spirit must become the directing force of all activities. Thus, the master is always in command of the self with strength, courage, and power to transcend the mind and manifest the will of the Spirit. Metaphorically, the master will maintain a steady rudder no matter the direction, force, or turbulence of the wind.

The force which animates life has a single purpose, which is shining its Light. Light that emerges from the Life Force is composed of Love and Truth. The purpose of physical life is to shine the light of the Spirit through the human body, thereby manifesting Love and Truth in the physical world. A master holds the power to shine this light in all its brilliance, unimpeded by the filters created by errors or karma. Every colour of the rainbow will radiate outwards through the cells of the human body. The aura of a human being is the sum total of all the emanations from within. When the intention is healing, the aura emanating from a master can change the aura of the subject, restoring the natural equilibrium between body, mind, and Spirit. During the process of meditation, prayer or healing, the aura of the Nazarene, the ancient master from biblical times, was so brilliant it extended outwards for approximately a kilometre.

Like true happiness, self-mastery is neither an objective nor a goal in this physical life. The purpose for being here on Earth is to shine the Light of the Life Force through the cells of the physical body in all its purity and brilliance. Self-mastery is the ability to radiate the Light of the Life Force in all its purity and brilliance. The journey that leads to self-mastery is mapped by the Light Force during meditations. These are the meditations that lead to the journey into Light.

One of the words that describe the transformation that takes place when all errors are erased or karma dissolved is "transfiguration". *"And as he prayed, the fashion of his countenance was altered, and his raiment was white and glistering." (Luke 9:29, Holy Bible, King James Version).* *"And after six days Jesus taketh Peter, James, and John his brother, and bringeth them up into an high mountain apart, And was transfigured before them: and his face did shine as the sun, and his raiment was white as the light." (Matthew 17:1-3, Holy Bible, King James Version).* There are other words that describe transformation such as Nirvana, Moksha, or Kaivalya. The process of transformation however is not sectarian but simply the way and the Truth of existence which applies to all.

As the transformed is no longer connected to this physical world due to the karma that links the Light Force to carbon-based incarnations, the realm of existence is now an open book. Some choose to return as teachers or guides. For example, the Nazarene master demonstrated the process of transformation using his life as the pattern to follow. Others choose different paths moving onward and upward as beings of Light. All of existence becomes an open book with vast treasures held within its pages. Amen.

Afterword
About Books of Interest

Books offer insight into a world that is seen through the eyes of the author. To the avid reader, books are like magic. The phrase, "open sesame" in the story of *Ali Baba and the Forty Thieves*, opens the mouth of a cave filled with treasure. To the avid reader, books contain a treasure that is revealed by the magic of words. Travel to faraway places, meet famous people, drive exotic cars, have romantic adventures, bathe in the most beautiful beaches, feast on the most delicious foods, travel back in time or forward into the future, visit other planets, worlds and realms. Nothing is impossible when words spark the imagination.

Looking back through my eyes when I was a child, I was attracted to spirituality from a very early age. Not being an avid reader, my mind was sparked from within. The *Holy Bible* felt like a magical book where eternal truths about life could be found. Eternal truths reveal an unseen and sacred world. I believed that entering the sanctuary of a church brought one closer to a place where eternal truths could be found. There was a deep emotional desire to find and understand the truth about life. I had many questions and quickly learnt that teachers and leaders from within the church were not the source of answers. Instead, they offered verses from the *Holy Bible* which they did not fully understand. I realized that obtaining truth had to come from a different source. At that time in my life, it was a conundrum in my mind. I did not realize I had to find it from within myself.

In my late teens, I left my home on the island of Trinidad in the Caribbean. I travelled thousands of miles and ended up studying Computer Science at the University of Guelph, in Ontario, Canada. Computer technology was new and daunting, but based on logic. I had a logical mind, and consequently excelled in mathematics and science. At university, the search for truth remained at the back of my mind as I explored subjects such as Algol, Cobol, Assembler, Fortran, and other computer hardware and software technologies.

On a personal level, it was a time when science and spirituality were viewed as a conflicting combination within social circles. The subject of spirituality, truth, and the inner world of the Life Force were seen as taboo and my thoughts and interests had to be kept to myself. Today however, spirituality can be found in the mainstream of society with expanding communities such as lightworkers.orgon the internet and Lily Dale Spiritualist Community in Cassadaga, New York—but back to my story.

I loved science and I loved to fix things, so these became the main focus of my academic, social and economic life. Spirituality remained in the background until I came across an aisle at the university library where books on the subjects of religion, spirituality, and the occult were shelved. The books were very interesting. One, on the works of Edgar Cayce, caught my attention. The words held an amazing treasure that sparked a journey which changed my life.

I had always enjoyed working with my hands as opposed to reading, until I discovered books written about the works of Edgar Cayce. They offered answers to questions that plagued my mind since childhood. I read every book in the library on the subject, then searched local bookstores, and bought all the books I could find on the subject. Today, my library holds about a hundred books on the works of Edgar Cayce and probably a hundred more on the topic of spiritual growth.

The four years at university brought a few changes in my focus due to distractions from socializing with friends, the introduction to alcohol, travel, exotic foods, and so on. My journey took some meandering turns, but the focus always returned to spiritual growth and the search for eternal truths about life.

I later discovered an organization that was founded by Edgar Cayce in 1931, called the A.R.E. (Association for Research and Enlightenment). Its purpose was helping people in a way that would transform their lives. The headquarters is located in Virginia Beach, Virginia, USA, and still exists today. I visited the headquarters on more than one occasion, had the opportunity to sit in their meditation room and experience the amazing depth of silence the setting offered. The location of the A.R.E. headquarters was chosen by Edgar Cayce. Many of my books came from the bookstore at the A.R.E. headquarters.

After getting married and living in an urban setting, one of my dreams was moving to the country. This was fulfilled when we purchased a house on five acres of land in Puslinch, Ontario. My heart always yearned for wide open spaces, the magic of the sunrise, expansive blue skies, and the peace and silence offered by a natural setting. Early morning walks allowed me to experience the burst of colour as the day awakened to the sunrise. It filled my heart with such joy to see and feel the excitement of the animals and birds as they sing and dance to welcome the dawn of a new day.

In the middle of the day, the silence and peacefulness of nature could be felt with every gust of the gentle breezes swishing through the tall green grass and into the open windows of the house, caressing my mind with a soft and gentle feeling of Love. Domed above a landscape from horizon to horizon, the blue light filtering down from unending skies exuded a feeling of Truth.

Such calls from nature entice the mind to become receptive and open to the creative peacefulness offered by the surrounding energies of the light, wind, sky and earth. Together, these create an environment conducive to meditation, contemplation, and exploration of the inner world of the Life Force. In the middle of the day, when these conditions presented themselves, I would use the opportunity to explore the treasures offered within the pages of books.

Preparing the mind to be receptive is like preparing for meditation. First, I would cleanse (shower, clean, wear comfortable clothes), and then find a place where the energy offered by nature could be felt, and open my mind to the treasure flowing from the pages of a book.

After exhausting topics found in the Edgar Cayce material, I explored writings from other authors such as Jane Roberts, T. Lobsang Rampa, and many, many others. I would explore the pathways described by the author as they etched new concepts on the walls of my mind, and hoped they would spark new insights that precipitate personal growth, until one day ...

These are some of the books that attracted my attention, during the early stages of my journey.

1. Allen, Eula, *Before the Beginning*, A.R.E. Press, Virginia Beach, Virginia, USA, 1976.

2. Association for Research and Enlightenment, Inc., *The New Complete Edgar Cayce Readings,* Edgar Cayce Foundation, Virginia Beach, Virginia, USA, 1973.

3. Baker, M. E. Penny, *Meditation, A Step Beyond with Edgar Cayce*, Pinnacle Books, N. Y., USA, 1975.

4. Bro, Harmon Hartzell, *Dreams in the Life of Prayer,* Harper and Row, N.Y., USA, 1970.

5. Bro, Harmon Hartzell, *Edgar Cayce on Dreams*, Warner Paperback Library, N.Y., USA, 1968.

6. Bro, Harmon Hartzell, *High Play*, Coward-Mc-Cann & Geoghegan Inc., N.Y., USA, 1971.

7. Dowling, Levi, *The Aquarian Gospel of Jesus the Christ,* Adventures Unlimited Press, Illinois, USA, 1996.

8. Furst, Jeffrey, *Edgar Cayce's Story of Attitudes and Emotions*, Berkley Publishing Corporation, N.Y., USA, 1974.

9. Furst, Jeffrey, *Edgar Cayce's Story of Jesus*, Coward Mc-Cann, Inc., N.Y., USA, 1970.

10. Herman, Ronna, *On Wings of Light*, Sunstar Publishing Ltd., 1996.

11. Huffman, Grace, *Affirmations for every day of the year*, A.R.E. Press, Virginia Beach, Virginia, USA, 1963.

12. Kittler, Glen D., *Edgar Cayce on the Dead Sea Scrolls*, Warner Paperback Library, N.Y., USA, 1973.

13. Klein, Eric, *Sacred Journey*, Medicine Bear Publishing, Blue Hill, Maine, USA, 1998.

14. Meurois-Givaudan, Anne and Daniel, *The Way of the Essenes*, Destiny Books, Rochester, Vermont, USA, 1993.

15. Puryear, Herbert B., Thurston, Mark A., *Meditation and the Mind of Man*, A.R.E. Press, Virginia Beach, Virginia, USA, 1975.

16. Puryear, Meredith Ann, *Healing through Meditation and Prayer*, A.R.E. Press, Virginia Beach, Virginia, USA, 1978.

17. Rampa, T. Lobsang, *The Third Eye,* Ballantine Books, N.Y. USA, 1964.

18. Roberts, Jane, *The Coming of Seth,* Simon & Schuster of Canada Ltd., Ontario, Canada, 1976.

19. Roman, Sanaya, and Packer, Duane, *Opening to Channel*, H. J. Kramer Inc., California, USA, 1989.

20. Sanderfur, Glenn, *Lives of the Master*, A.R.E. Press, Virginia Beach, Virginia, USA, 1998.

21. Schiffmann, Erich, *Yoga – The Spirit and Practice of Moving into Stillness*, Pocket Books, New York, USA, 1996.

22. Sechrist, Elsie, *Meditation: Gateway to Light*, A.R.E. Press, Virginia Beach, Virginia, USA, 1972.

23. Sparrow, Lynn, *Meditation Made Easy*, Edgar Cayce Foundation, Virginia Beach, Virginia, USA, 1999.

24. Canadian Bible Society, The *Holy Bible*,

University Press, Oxford, GB, 1972.

25. Winston, Shirley Rabb, *Music as the Bridge*, A.R.E. Press, Virginia Beach, Virginia, USA, 1972.

26. Woodward, Mary Ann, *Be Still and Know*, A.R.E. Press, Virginia Beach, Virginia, USA, 1968.

... Until one day, while deep in contemplative thought, the realization came to me that books were only a source of knowledge and not a pathway which led to Truth or personal growth. Knowledge must first be lived to become personal Truth. Knowledge must resonate with the Life Force within in order to integrate with the psyche. The process of reading words was insufficient. It would not provide the method for revealing the treasure. Knowledge without experience would simply clutter the mind with words and ideas, and furthermore, would filter out Light seeking to spark new thoughts (inspiration and intuition).

I remember the day very clearly. I was overcome with this realization when preparing to read. It became so clear in my mind that growth comes from manifesting thoughts that were sparked by Light shining from above, rather than from the pages of books. The magical treasure (Truth) can only be revealed by the Light of the Life Force. With this realization, I felt that books were no longer necessary for my journey and had to be silenced. I stopped reading and instead explored this new pathway. When there were moments energized by nature, I would open my mind to the inner world of the Life Force through meditation.

Meditation was not simply sitting for a period of time and musing. I was committed to finding the pathway to the inner world of the Life Force. Sometimes I would spend two hours each day, one hour before dawn and another in the afternoon, meditating. These were times of the day when the peace and calm offered by nature felt the strongest. During meditation, I felt connected to something greater than myself. After each session, my mind felt energized by the Love and Truth flowing from the inner world. My mind felt focused. My heart felt energized. I was ready to face the world, armed with Love and Truth. I continued with the practice, not knowing what more to expect, until early one morning while deep in meditation, I saw the image of a large winged figure descend from above, and stand just outside the room looking in at me through the wall of glass. Within the silence, only shades of grey were visible. The image appeared for only a brief moment.

The unexpected appearance jolted my mind out of the meditative silence, and back to physical consciousness, which caused the image to disappear. I believe it was a visitation from the angel, Gabriel, the one that appeared during biblical times. At first,

I was disappointed by my reaction which caused the disappearance, but later realized that the experience validated the existence of an active inner world, one that is accessible by anyone through meditation. I realized that we are not alone on our journey. The emergence of the angel Gabriel from this place was an important milestone on my path. This was at an early stage of a long journey into the Light which shines from within the inner world of the Life Force.

The appearance of the angel Gabriel was not the first nor the last experience that validated the existence of an expansive world that envelopes the life experienced as physical reality. There is a unique path for each person, one that leads to the Light of the Life Force which shines from within the inner world. Personal experience showed me that this path can be found with a commitment to the practice of meditation.

It is my hope that this book will serve as a treasure map that leads to the inner world. Once the path is discovered, what happens next is up to you. When choices are based on Love and Truth, you will be guided towards the Light of the inner world. Do not be afraid if mystical experiences occur along the way. It is only natural.

The purpose of life here on Earth is not about mystical experiences. It is about finding and following the path that connects both worlds. The master has discovered that this path lives in both worlds. Amen.

Dawn

It is early in the morning.
The sky blinks and wipes her eyes.
Then she smiles,
Her smile so radiant.
The world awakens to behold her beauty.
Her gentle eyes blink slowly
As she looks down upon me
In silent pleasure.
Her freckled face glows.
Like an angel, her hair lights up.
And my mind wanders,
Away to the distant horizon.
To embrace such beauty,
That only God can create.
Sunrise!

Embrace the totality of life here on Earth and beyond by walking through that door opened only by a master, into the dawn of a new existence.

APPENDIX A
The Life Force Chart

Relationship Between the Life Force and the Human Body								
No.	Chakra	Endocrine	Colour	Purpose	Emotions and Feelings	Intention	Positive Feelings	Negative Feelings
7	Crown	Pituitary	Violet	Enlightenment	Connection with the Life Force, Empowerment, Advancement	Manifest happiness through all the chakras	Faith in Life	Ego, Attachments
6	Third Eye	Pineal	Indigo	Perception	Intuition	Trust in inner feelings	Satisfaction	Doubt, Mistrust Self, Illusion
5	Throat	Thyroid	Blue	Communicating One's Truth	Self Determination, Communication Between Chakras	Manifest inner Truth	Truth	Self-Denial, Lies
4	Heart	Thymus	Green	Compassion	Healing, Forgiveness	Inject Love in all situations	Compassion	Grief, Sadness, Fear
3	Solar Plexus	Adrenal	Yellow	Empowerment	Mental Energy, Self-Esteem, Personal Power, Courage	Manifest the three chakras above without fear.	Will Power	Shame, Self-Denial, Fear
2	Sacral	Lyden	Orange	Fertility	Emotion, Sensuality	Manifest the three chakras above using creative energy.	Innovation	Destructive, Guilt, Fear
1	Root	Gonads	Red	Evolution	Sense of belonging, well-being, Safety	Feel a sense of belonging with sufficient to survive in safety.	Fight, Flight, Self-Preservation	Greed, Over-Indulgence, Fear

APPENDIX B
Exercises

When the intention is the change that emerges from the practice of meditation, a commitment to simple but powerful exercises will have a huge impact on the nature of one's life. It is not necessary to perform all of them simultaneously. Choose one or two which offer the greatest benefit and practice them with a commitment to self.

Exercise One – Planting Intentions

Before falling asleep, lie on your back with palms crossed over the navel and relax, allowing your body to sink into the bed by releasing all the muscles. It will feel like you are floating. When this occurs, review intentions you wish to hold within each energy centre, starting from the root all the way to the crown. Then, allow yourself to drift into sleep.

During sleep, the Life Force will integrate intentions with the subconscious.

Exercise Two – Natural Rhythms

Practice waking up each day without an alarm. Start this exercise by setting your intention to wake up at a certain time. Hold this intention before going to bed. For example, it may be a time to experience the sunrise, go for a walk, write in a journal, or meditate. Have sufficient time to complete an activity unrelated to work or home life, something for self. At first, waking up will be difficult. The body will easily assume old patterns. With practice however, the body will become self-aware shortly before the alarm is activated. You will have the opportunity to turn it off before it aggravates your consciousness.

This exercise will reawaken the natural rhythm or cycles of the human body and set the pace for the day ahead.

Exercise Three – Set Intentions

Before stirring the body, as you become self-aware after sleeping, review your dreams. Then, review the intentions you wish to hold within each chakra and plan to apply them in situations encountered during the day.

This exercise will help you remember your dreams. Take some time to write them down before leaving your bed. During the day, reflect upon your dreams, expecting that answers will emerge. Observe as different attitudes are interjected into situations.

Exercise Four – Remember Happiness

Recall a time in life when the greatest form of happiness was experienced. It may be the result of a dream, walking by the seaside, watching a thunderstorm, contemplating in a sacred place, or during meditation. Set a timer to alert you once every hour of the day, and in that moment, recall that state of happiness.

This exercise will remind the whole being that there is something greater than the tangible. Hormones will be released in the blood steam which will result in positive change.

Exercise Five – Choose Happiness

Upon becoming self-aware when emerging from sleep, choose happiness as the first and foremost directing force in life. Hold the attitude that each intention and action will be predicated upon happiness. For example, take time to view the sunrise and allow its magnificence and beauty to fill the consciousness with happiness. Enter into each situation with this state of mind. Realize that everything else is secondary to maintaining this state of being. Jobs, family, friends, and material possessions are all secondary. However, recognize that the happiness stored within will overflow onto all situations in life in the form of Love and Truth. This would apply to jobs, family, friends, and material possessions. In preparation for this exercise, reflect upon the beauty and happiness conveyed by the words of the poem entitled *Dawn*, found at the end of part twenty-four.

By recalling this natural state, this exercise will help set the intention to create a path that leads back to that place.

Exercise Six – Reveal Karma

After five hours of sleep, arise. For a period of about five minutes, appeal to the Life Force within to bring the changes in your life which you desire. For example, to be able to objectively observe oneself and see one's true nature, or to manifest Love and Truth without condition or expectation. Then, practice meditation for fifteen minutes. Return to bed and sleep for three more hours.

This exercise incubates dreams and reveals karmic ties.

Exercise Seven – Daily Prayer

Before each meal, take a moment to reflect upon the attitude you wish to hold within the heart chakra. Choose Love as the transforming intention in all interactions. After each meal, contemplate with an attitude of expectancy. This will activate the third and fifth chakras.

With this exercise, the body will be nourished as needed, in order to manifest intentions.

Exercise Eight – Walk Each Day

Upon rising each day and without fail, walk twenty minutes. Do not rush. Do not use electronics. Swing your hands freely and comfortably back and forth. Find something to enjoy about being alone in a natural environment, such as the sunrise or the singing of the birds. Do this whether it is raining, snowing, cold, or warm. Do this if you are at home or travelling.

On the path that emerges from the practice of meditation, maintaining a healthy lifestyle will always be an asset. A walk each day will benefit both the mental and physical.

Exercise Nine – Planting Light Buds

Each day, focus the intention upon a word or phrase that resonates with personal aspirations. If you do not have one, choose from the list of "Light Buds" in *Appendix C*.

If you choose to nurture it, it will enlighten your life and blossom into happiness.

Exercise Ten – Daily Meditation

Without fail, meditate at least twice each day, once before starting the day and then before retiring at the end of the day. Enter into the practice with an attitude expecting that life's journey will always manifest the light of Love and Truth regardless of the situation or circumstance.

This practice will open the door to the indwelling Life Force and keep it open.

Appendix C
Light Buds

Each day, focus your intention on a word or phrase that resonates with your aspirations. If you choose to nurture it, it will enlighten your life and happiness will blossom.

1. Meditation can be used to access the dynamics of life and make changes to restore the equilibrium between the Life Force and the mind, body, psyche, and consciousness.

2. Love is recognizing that all are imperfect while helping others on their journey towards perfection.

3. Worship in body, mind, and Spirit. Worship the Spirit, direct the mind, and command the body.

4. It is natural to ask, "What comes after death?" Birth seems like an unnatural answer but it is the Truth.

5. Each person is unique, thus, the journey of life will be unique.

6. When you look at a person, what do you see first? The mind, spirit, or body?

7. Creativity is a function of Love.

8. Peace is a function of Love.

9. Love thrives in a relationship where the mutual freedom of self-expression is honoured.

10. What is the most valuable item one can possess? It is the human body. It is the instrument which enables experience in the physical reality. Without it, you are naught.

11. Love recognizes the capacity within each of us to make errors and offers the opportunity to erase them.

12. You really don't know who you are or what you are capable of until you are in touch with your Spirit.

13. Change the world, one person at a time, as a living example.

14. We are all brothers and sisters of the same mother, the earth.

15. What is a true church? It is a place where eternal Truths offer a pathway back to the true self.

16. You are the result of your choices.

17. Practice recognizing where thoughts come from: the indwelling spirit or external forces. Use this knowledge to determine whether to act or to let the thought go.

18. As the sun lights the earth at sunrise, so too does the Spirit fill the body.

19. The purpose of being here in this realm is to destroy our house one brick at a time (psyche) and rebuild it upon the rock of Truth using Love as the cement.

20. At times of challenge, go within and find the place of balance. It is the place where life is resonating with Love and Truth.

21. Know the feeling of being in balance. Know when you are not in balance and know how to restore it through meditation.

22. When you listen, when you choose, the voice you want to hear is that of the Spirit within.

23. I AM in command, not fear.

24. Free the mind from the busyness of the world and let it become silent in order to hear the voice of the Spirit. Let this voice be a guiding light.

25. The body is from the earth. The Life Force which animates the body is from the realms beyond.

26. Human life is the result of the body and Spirit existing as one. Honour both.

27. The body is part of the ecosystem of the planet. Adding poison to the planet is adding poison to your body.

28. Mind is the builder, thus, command the mind to build a new life founded upon Love and Truth.

29. You will not know what you are capable of until challenged.

30. The only one you have the power to change is

yourself.

31. The greatest challenger one will face is the self.

32. Self-determination starts when one can truly step aside, look at self objectively, and use the opportunity to make different choices.

33. Realize that you are Spirit first.

34. Do not let tiredness, hunger, illness, peer pressure, or any form of weakness dictate choices and actions. Instead let the indwelling Spirit be the guiding influence.

35. Why is there so much love for the material world when we should seek the Love that emerges from the Light which animates our life?

36. During the practice of meditation, plant seeds in the mind which blossom into Truth and Love.

37. Find the person you want to be and nurture it.

38. All of us have the same powerful potential.

39. Sometimes we forget who we are and identify

only with the material. Looking through the eyes of Love and Truth will remind us who we truly are—beings of Light.

40. Each person holds the power to change a life: their own.

41. The journey of life is about unravelling the self and re-knitting a new being, one that is based on eternal Truths.

42. Walk into the light of your Spirit and your days on Earth may always be enlightened.

43. When spirits intertwine, it is like chords of music playing a beautiful harmony that exudes the joy of Love and Truth.

44. The mind is unaware of so much which impacts its life.

45. This physical body is an instrument of Light which is used to experience a slice of time within the landscape of eternity.

46. Meditation is a way to tap into the engineering of life. Becoming adept means becoming an engineer who can adjust the internal mechanics for greater efficiency. Efficiency

means life is operating as designed.

47. True freedom lies in the capacity to recognize the power of the free will within and the ability to use it for self-direction in life.

48. Happiness is the natural state to be aspired to. It is in the blueprint of the subconscious.

49. The end therefore is the beginning, and the beginning, the end.

50. Choices made in the past defined the past. The future is an open book with stories you will write.

BIBLIOGRAPHY

Association for Research and Enlightenment, Inc., *The New Complete Edgar Cayce Readings*, Edgar Cayce Foundation, Virginia Beach, Virginia, USA, 1973, Readings 549-1, 281-13.

Buddha Dharma Education Association Inc., *Guide to Tipitaka*, Burma, 1985,

https://www.buddhanet.net/pdf_file/tipitaka.pdf, Chapter III, pp. 34-39.

Devi, Parama Karuna, *Bhagavad Gita*, Jagannatha Vallabha Vedic Research Center, Odisha, India, 2016, pp. 160.

Haleem, M. A. S. Abdel, *The Qur'an*, Oxford University Press, New York, USA, 2005.

Project Gutenberg, *Alibaba and the Forty Thieves*, USA, 2011,

https://www.gutenberg.org/files/37679/37679-h/37679-h.htm.

Project Gutenberg, The *Holy Bible*, King James Version, USA, 1992, https://www.gutenberg.org/ebooks/10, 1 Corinthians 13:1, 1 Corinthians 15:55-56, 1 John 4:18, 1 John 5:4, 1 Samuel 3:10, Acts 2:2-4, Ecclesiastes 1:1, Exodus 3:14, Genesis 1:2, Genesis 2:16-17, Genesis 3:6, Genesis 28:10-32, John 5:8, John 14:16-18, John 18:38, Luke 11:4, Mark 4:39, Mark, 8:34, Matthew 5:15, Matthew 6:12, Matthew, 9:9, Proverbs 15:1, Psalm 23:4, Psalm 27:3, Psalm 103:1-5, Romans 3:23.

Saraswati, Chandrasekharendra, *The Vedas*, Siddhi Printers. Mumbai, India, 1998, pp. 29, 34, 64, 80, 85.

Singh, Karan, *Mundaka Upanishad*, Bharatiya Vidya Bhavan, Bombay, India, 1987. pp. 22, 57, 75, 76.

The End

The time has come.
The journey into Light is at the end.

Love has been mastered.

Life has been rebuilt upon
A foundation of Truth.

Go forth into the world

Knowing,

The student has become

A master,

A light and an example,
The true role of a teacher.

Go forth into the beyond

Knowing

You have freed yourself.

You are no longer
Fettered to this world.

Amen.

www.ingramcontent.com/pod-product-compliance
Lightning Source LLC
Chambersburg PA
CBHW060151050426
42446CB00013B/2772